The Trainee Primary Teacher's Handbook

Also available from Continuum

The Trainee Teacher's Survival Guide (2nd edition),
   Hazel Bennett

The Trainee Secondary Teacher's Handbook, Gererd Dixie

100 Ideas for Trainee Teachers, Angella Cooze

Getting the Buggers to Behave (3rd edition), Sue Cowley

How to Survive Your First Year in Teaching (2nd edition),
   Sue Cowley

The Trainee Primary Teacher's Handbook

Gererd Dixie and Janet Bell

continuum

Continuum International Publishing Group

The Tower Building	80 Maiden Lane
11 York Road	Suite 704
London	New York
SE1 7NX	NY 10038

www.continuumbooks.com

Cartoons drawn by Peter Rennoldson | peter@bigcarrot.co.uk

British Library Cataloguing-in-Publication Data
A catalogue record for this book is available from the British Library.

ISBN: 978-0826-418388 (paperback)

Library of Congress Cataloguing-in-Publication Data

Dixie, Gererd.
  The trainee primary teacher's handbook / Gererd Dixie and Janet Bell.
    p. cm.

Includes bibliographical references.
ISBN 978-0-8264-1838-8 (pbk. : alk. paper) 1. Elementary school teachers--Training of--Great Britain. 2. Elementary school teaching--Vocational guidance--Great Britain. I. Bell, Janet, 1961- II. Title.

LB1776.4.G7D59 2009
370.71'141--dc22

2009008465

Typeset by Ben Cracknell Studios | www.benstudios.co.uk
Printed and bound in Great Britain by Bell and Bain Ltd, Glasgow

Mixed Sources
Product group from well-managed
forests and other controlled sources
www.fsc.org Cert no. TT-COC-002769
© 1996 Forest Stewardship Council

Contents

List of abbreviations

ADD	Attention-Deficit Disorder
ADHD	Attention-Deficit Hyperactivity Disorder
AfL	Assessment for Learning
ASDs	Autistic Spectrum Disorders
AST	Advanced Skills Teacher
BEd.	Bachelor of Education
CAT	Credit and Accumulation Transfer Scheme
CEDP	Career Entry and Development Profile
DCFS	Department for Children, Families and Schools
DipHE	Diploma in Higher Education
DRB	Designated Recommending Body
EAL	English as an Additional Language
EBITT	Employment-Based Initial Teacher Training
G and T	Gifted and Talented
GTC	General Teaching Council
GTP	Graduate Teacher Programme
GTTR	Graduate Teacher Training Registry
HAPs	Higher-Ability Pupils
HEI	Higher Educational Institutions
HND	Higher National Diploma
ICT	Information Communication Technology
IEP	Individual Education Plan
ITT	Initial Teacher Training
KS	Key Stage
LA	local authority
LAPs	lower-ability pupils
LSA	Learning Support Assistant
MAPs	medium-ability pupils
NARIC	National Academic Recognition Centre
NC	National Curriculum
NQT	Newly Qualified Teacher
Ofsted	Office for Standards in Education
OTTP	Overseas Trained Teacher Programme
PGCE	Postgraduate Certificate in Education or Professional Graduate Certificate in Education
PPA	planning, preparation and assessment time

PRU	pupil referral unit
QCA	Qualification and Curriculum Authority
QTS	qualified teacher status
RTP	Registered Teacher Programme
SATs	Standard Assessment Tests
SCITT	School-Centred Initial Teacher Training
SEN	Special Educational Needs
SENCO	Special Needs Coordinator
SKfT	Subject Knowledge for Teaching
TA	teaching assistant
TDA	Training and Development Agency
TES	*Times Educational Supplement*
UCAS	Universities and Colleges Admissions Service
VLE	Virtual Learning Environment

Introduction

> To teach is to touch a life forever
>
> (Primary school staffroom)

We have both been involved in teacher training in one way or another for the last ten years, and find that there is no escape from talking about our work. All sorts of people want to speak to us about training to be a teacher. Sometimes it's about them, and sometimes it's about a friend, neighbour or relative. We have both had long phone conversations with strangers about what qualifications they need, how they can train and what they need to do next. We have met people at parties who want to escape from their dull jobs, and who seize the opportunity to explore the possibility of teaching, once they know what we do. We have talked with friends who finally admit that teaching is a burning ambition but they have not felt confident to pursue their dream. We are both still always glad to speak about teaching, which we believe is the best profession in the world, but rarely feel we can give all the information required in a short chat. This book is our opportunity to write it all down so that anyone can access it.

The initial purpose of it is to furnish you with the information, guidance and advice you will need to make an informed decision about whether to teach or not. Then, we will explore the nature of teacher training, if you decide to apply for a course. If you are forewarned about the expectations and experiences you are likely to encounter during your training, you will be able to make the necessary practical, emotional and academic preparations that are fundamental to you in being able to make a successful start to your course.

The book is divided into seven parts, six of which represent your training needs at various points along a chronological continuum, from the point at which you first started to think about teaching as a career right through to the end of your training (Figure 1:1). It should be

Your journey through this handbook

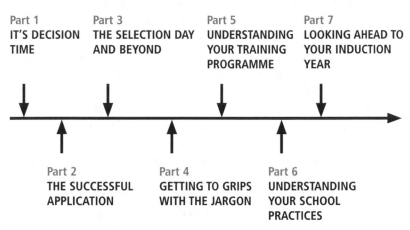

Figure 1 The teacher-training continuum

stressed at the very outset that the advice and guidance offered within this book is generic in nature and will not meet all your subject-specific needs. Having said this, however, a chapter on how to gain, develop and utilize your subject knowledge has been included in Part 5. We have outlined the various parts below in textual and diagrammatic form so that you gain an understanding of the sequential nature of the chapters.

- Part 1   It's Decision Time
- Part 2   The Successful Application
- Part 3   Preparing for the Selection Day and Beyond
- Part 4   Getting to Grips with the Jargon
- Part 5   Understanding your Training Programme
- Part 6   Understanding your School Practices
- Part 7   Looking Ahead to your Induction Year

The three chapters in Part 1, It's Decision Time, have been written with those early decisions in mind. Chapter 1 explores your initial exploratory thoughts about teaching and offers you guidance on how to find out whether your dreams of becoming a teacher meet the reality of life in a modern-day primary school. Chapter 2 provides you with guidance on visiting schools and on how to conduct additional research in an attempt to discover realistic scenarios about teaching. It is hoped that from these you will be able to make informed decisions about whether or not to go through with the application process. Chapter 3 takes the process one step further by furnishing you with a range of different routes into teacher training. This will be followed by an exploration of the pros and cons of each initial teacher-training (ITT) programme. In doing this we hope to afford you the opportunity to match your ability, personality, personal background and/or dominant learning styles with an appropriate course. Some consideration will also be given to the pre-course requirements associated with each of these ITT programmes.

We have entitled Part 2 The Successful Application because the purpose of all three chapters is to provide you with advice and guidance about what to do once you have decided to apply for an ITT course. Having chosen your preferred teacher-training route, you need to think about the nature of the application process itself. Chapter 4 offers advice on how to use your pre-course school visits to full effect before then going on to explain how you can use this information to support your application. Chapter 5 provides detailed guidance on how to use your lesson observations to explore a range of teaching styles and how to gain a rudimentary understanding of the behaviour management strategies used in primary schools today. A detailed exploration of the preparatory work required for a successful interview will then take place. In Chapter 6 we go on to show you how to complete your application form successfully and write a personal statement.

Two of the chapters in Part 3 provide you with guidance on how to perform well on the training course selection day. We use the term 'selection day' rather than 'interview day' because we need to make it clear to you that your assessment will not merely be confined to your performance in the formal interview. Chapter 7 focuses on the selection tasks you will have to complete before, during and/or after the selection day, while Chapter 8 provides you with detailed guidance about how to perform well in the interview itself. On the assumption that your application has been successful, Chapter 9 goes on to offer a full exploration of the pre-course preparations you are advised to make in order to enjoy a successful training period. In addition to this, it also helps you to gain a fuller understanding of the functions and roles of education, the school and teacher.

One of the things you will be confronted with during the initial few days of your first school visit is a huge amount of educational jargon used on a daily basis. What is meant by the terms SENCO, EAL, SATs? What exactly is differentiation? Part 4, Getting to Grips with the Jargon, consists of only one chapter (Chapter 10) and is selective in offering you an exploration of some of the educational terms and issues that you are highly likely to come across during your training. This chapter has been produced to enable you to become familiar with the language of teaching.

Part 5, Understanding your Training Programme, focuses on the principles of teacher training and on the requirements of your specific training programme. The part starts with Chapter 11 which describes some of the issues that may arise during a very busy year. This chapter affords you an opportunity to explore these issues and, in doing so, it will provide you with an indication of the training journey ahead. Chapter 12 goes on to offer advice and guidance designed to help you get to know, and meet, the professional standards for qualified teacher status (QTS). Chapter 13 highlights the need for IIT you to show an understanding of the principles of reflective practice and to be able to use this to inform your training and teaching. All teacher-training providers will require you to complete academic work to support your professional practice. Chapters 14 and 15 have been designed to help you to get the most out of your presentations, workshops and lectures, and to provide guidance on how to write good assignments and essays. Bearing in mind the high status afforded by the Training and Development Agency (TDA) to the importance of subject knowledge, Chapter 16 has been written to help you to improve and demonstrate your subject knowledge for teaching.

Finally the moment has arrived – you are ready to start your first school practice. Part 6, Understanding Your School Practices, consists of 14 chapters which explore a range of issues relating to your time in school.

Part 7, Looking Ahead to your Induction Year, comprises seven chapters, all of which have been written to support your move towards newly qualified teacher (NQT) status. Chapter 31 explores some of the social, philosophical and practical issues you will have to think about when deciding which type of school you intend to apply to. Chapter 32 provides in-depth guidance on how to write a good letter of application and what you can do should you get towards the end of your training and still not have a job. Chapter 33 will provide you with some top tips to help to you stay one step ahead of the game in the selection process and to support a successful application for your first teaching post. As is pointed out in Chapter 3, making an impression on children and staff is a requisite ingredient of any successful job application. Chapter 34 explores the ways in which you can use your personality and interpersonal skills to make an impression on those involved in the selection process. Bearing in mind that it is highly likely that you will have to teach a specimen lesson on your selection day, Chapter 35 provides you with useful top tips to consider when planning this lesson. And then there is the interview itself. In the same format as that presented to you in your ITT interview guidance, Chapter 36 provides a range of advice on how to perform well at interview. This is supported by a menu of potential interview questions and model answers. Finally, to prepare you for what is likely to be one of your final tasks as an ITT trainee, Chapter 37 explores the role of the Career Entry and Development Profile, and offers you guidance on how to complete this in an effective and productive manner.

How you choose to use this book is entirely up to you. You might, for example, prefer to read it from cover to cover in order to gain an overall picture of the themes, issues and practices relevant to your training. Alternatively, you may wish to focus on the specific chapters that are most representative of your needs at any given point along the training continuum. However you decide to use this book, we are hopeful and confident that it will fulfil its role as originally envisaged when we first put pen to paper – that of acting as a supportive, informative and critical friend throughout your training. With this in mind we would like to wish you all the very best for the journey ahead.

Part One
IT'S DECISION TIME

Early thoughts

It is true to say that teachers start their career journeys in very different ways. For a small number of people, the process of thinking about becoming a teacher is almost revelatory, a 'light bulb' moment that helped to illuminate the new career path ahead of them. However, for the vast majority of people, the process starts with an initial 'germ' of a thought which grows exponentially until it eventually becomes 'all-consuming' in nature. Many of the trainee teachers we work with describe how they have always wanted to teach, and have progressively become more involved with working with children through their school and university education. They remember playing 'schools', babysitting, helping out at Sunday school, or running Brownie and Cub groups. Others describe how they started to think about teaching as a career as a result of being extremely unhappy in their current job or because they were simply desperate for a new sense of direction. Others felt less strongly about their circumstances. They certainly did not experience a sense of dread when getting up for work in the morning, but felt that they were simply coasting through life without any real sense of purpose. Through volunteer work with children, they found a new direction and wanted real job satisfaction.

Our conversations with numerous trainees and qualified teachers over the past ten years have often demonstrated the importance of those early schooldays in influencing their decisions to become teachers. During this initial exploratory phase their thoughts often drifted back to their own schooldays, to those teachers who had inspired them to greater things, or conversely to those teachers who had demotivated them or humiliated them in front of their peers. Either way there is no doubt that the quality of teaching they experienced as children has had a dramatic effect upon their decision to become teachers.

We have both explored this issue with trainees over the years and have asked them to use reflective journals to write about the teachers who inspired them. We have discovered that the memories of the trainees of their own school lives have played a significant role in their decision to become teachers. In deciding to take up the profession, they had drawn upon these experiences, both positive and negative, to inform their decision as to what type of teacher they would like to aspire to be. In all cases an overwhelming desire to 'make a difference' was displayed. We are sure that you will empathize with some of the feelings expressed in the quotes shown below by trainees following the Suffolk and Norfolk Primary SCITT programme.

> I remember Mrs X with great affection as she was a brilliant role model and someone who inspired me. She was extremely calm and kind, although you knew what would happen if you misbehaved. I made that mistake once and once only! She also took a great interest in all of her children's lives. She would always ask about my dance exams and performances which made me feel really special. Even now we still keep in touch at Christmas. I have spoken to her regarding my training and she has been extremely supportive, just as she was 20 years ago.
>
> (Helen Smith, trainee)

> Mrs Y was the reason that I wanted to be a teacher. I was about ten years old and had survived school in a haze, doing the bare minimum and getting by. One day in maths, Mrs Y directly aimed a question at me, 'Go on', she said, 'You can do it.' I plucked up the courage to answer the question. 'Fantastic, well done', came the reply. My pride leapt, and from that day on my attitude to school changed. I went on to do a science degree. I want to give children that same sense of pride, to feel that their contribution is worthwhile, and to encourage them to make the most of their education, just as Mrs Y did for me.
>
> (Penny Dawson, trainee)

> During my own primary education I was fortunate enough to encounter several truly excellent teachers who really made the learning come alive for me. I mistook this for the norm, and I can remember my surprise when in high school, I came across peers who had detested those same years that I had cherished so much. I realized then and there that a child's primary education really can be defined by the individual practitioners they are placed with. I was one of the privileged few to be under the care of educators who unlocked my potential and showed me how to succeed. I wholeheartedly loved my primary years and have always felt that children of the future deserve to feel the same way about theirs; this is what made me want to become a teacher.
>
> (Jane Palmer, trainee)

It is fair to say that at this early stage of their teaching journey many potential trainees have a rather idealistic view of their role as future teachers. They have not yet realized that the skills and qualities demonstrated by their favourite teachers often involve a lot of soul-searching, a great deal of emotional turmoil and sheer hard work, and that these took many years to master. The very best teachers constantly strive to meet the highest of professional standards and attempt to hold the highest expectations of their children. It is fair to say, however, that in the hurly-burly of everyday school life, where teachers are often presented with scenarios that challenge this philosophy, it is often difficult to maintain this idealism. Although it is important never totally to lose this idealistic streak, you will need to temper this perspective with a degree of realism. In this initial exploratory stage of your journey it is important for you to find out what life in the modern-day primary school is really like. Before you make any decisions to apply for an ITT course you need to take the first steps to discover whether teaching really is for you. This chapter has been specifically written to help you to do just this.

So, what is teaching actually like? There is no doubt in our minds that teaching is a special calling. Both authors are privileged to have been part of the profession for the last 25 years and have found it to be the most challenging yet rewarding way to make a living. However, before you make any decisions about whether it is for you or not, you need to understand fully the demands of the job.

Teaching is a demanding career, physically, emotionally and intellectually. It calls for energy, dedication, patience and enthusiasm. This is all well and good when you are feeling physically well and emotionally strong, when you have had a good night's sleep and you and your family are not experiencing personal problems that are likely to impinge on your preparation and planning time. Teaching and the acting professions have a great deal in common. It does not matter what you feel like on the day: you have simply got to get up there and perform. It is not like a routine office job where you can sit in the corner, nurse your hangover and get on with your paperwork without being disturbed. The children, quite rightly, will demand your full attention and commitment during their time with you, and will not usually let you get away with an under-par performance. In order to teach effectively you must have enthusiasm for each subject and be able to deliver your lessons in a confident and effective manner. Classroom-management skills are therefore essential. No matter how well you plan your lessons, things often go awry, so you do need the ability to be able to think on your feet. If you have the perception that teaching is a 'nine-to-five' job, and that you will be able to get back home in time to watch your favourite television programme, then please think again. There will be a lot of preparation and marking to do in the evenings and at weekends. All this calls for good time management, self-discipline, administration and organization, as well as good leadership skills. It sounds basic, but it is essential that you like and relate well to children and that you are committed to opening up young minds. You'll also need excellent communication skills, a keen intellect, creativity and bags of energy. Perhaps one of the most important qualities you will require as a teacher is that of 'reflectivity'. If you are highly sensitive to criticism, or if you have a tendency to be overconfident and think that you know all the answers, then teaching is certainly not the profession for you. Throughout your training you will receive a wealth of advice and guidance designed to improve your pedagogic practice. Even for the most experienced of us, this process can be quite uncomfortable at times. We will explore the reflective process in more detail in Chapter 13.

As indicated in the beginning of this part, there are many rewards that come with this career. As a teacher you will be afforded the privilege and opportunity to unlock the potential of the children in your classes. Although not each child will succeed academically, you should hold on to your beliefs that each one of them has the potential for success in one form or another. The onset of each new academic year presents new and exciting challenges and new potential successes, and we are sure that you can imagine the feeling of absolute euphoria when you have been instrumental in 'turning a challenging child around'.

You will never learn a topic better than when you start teaching it. It is highly likely that even the most conscientious of university graduates will initially be uncomfortable in teaching everything in the school's curriculum. The research and planning stages, so necessary for good teaching, will help you to gain more intimate subject knowledge and more importantly will provide you with the skills necessary to deliver this to your audience. It takes time to become a good teacher.

Despite a whole host of government and school-based initiatives, it is fair to say that once you qualify you will still be able to maintain a high degree of control over what goes on in your classroom. Very few jobs offer such scope for autonomy and creativity as teaching. Most teachers will tell you that it helps to have a sense of humour. A sense of humour is **absolutely essential** if you are going to be successful in establishing and maintaining good relationships with your children and in engaging them in the learning process. If you have a positive attitude and a sense of humour, you will find things to laugh about on an everyday basis. Children like teachers who smile and laugh with them. Recently there was a television advert sponsored by the Training and Development Agency (TDA) that encouraged people to think about teaching and 'to work with some of funniest people in the world'. This advert has got it absolutely right. Sometimes it will be jokes that kids share with you that give you the most pleasure, but mostly the opportunity for humour will arise from the spontaneity of your children who will make the funniest statements without realizing what they have said. It is important in your darkest hours in teaching to keep your sense of humour.

Many of you reading this book will have children and it cannot have escaped your notice that, on the face of it, the school calendar will allow you to have the same school time commitments as your offspring. There is no doubt that this is an added bonus to the job, but please be aware that you will have numerous meetings after school and that you will probably have to work some evenings. It is fair to say that this may create stress and will certainly impinge on your personal and family time. Having said this, there are plenty of opportunities for you to work part-time in the profession while you are bringing up your family. You may even wish to take up the opportunity to job-share in a school. It is possible to do this even during your NQT year, although this will of course affect the length of your induction period. The following quotation outlines one of the benefits of taking up such a flexible career:

> I qualified to teach 15 years ago when I was straight out of college and single. I enjoyed the challenges of the primary classroom but after a few years I took time off to travel around the world and had many amazing experiences. I came back and was able to supply teach at first, and then gained a permanent position. I had my son seven years ago and became part-time, job-sharing with a friend of mine. This has given me the flexibility to have time with Noah and continue my career. I now thoroughly enjoy being a mentor to trainees and am now taking on more responsibility within the SCITT programme by monitoring trainees in other schools, helping train mentors and interviewing applicants.
>
> (Vanessa Wood, primary teacher and lead ITT mentor)

The other thing you need to note is that some of the so-called holiday time will be used to prepare and mark children's work. Many teachers feel that the only 'real' break they get is the five-week holiday afforded to them during the summer. Even then they say that it takes a couple of weeks to 'wind down' and forget about school, albeit on a temporary basis. You also need to know that the holiday period is usually when many teachers often become unwell. Having been stoical in staving off illness during the course of term, they start to relax during the holiday period and, as a result of doing so, often come down with coughs and colds and the like. Once the adrenaline stops pumping, your body seems to succumb to illness.

If your partner is not a teacher, you both need to be very clear about the possible impact of your new career on your relationship and on your life-style. Bearing in mind that you will have a great deal of marking and preparatory work to do, they will have to get used to the idea that they might be seeing a lot less of you during term time, and that you will not be able to take holidays during the school term. This also means that you will no longer be able to choose the cheapest times to go on holiday. Be prepared for a substantial increase in travel and accommodation costs during the school breaks.

The Training and Development Agency is committed to promoting diversity in the teaching profession and is keen to make it more representative of society as a whole. It openly welcomes applications from under-represented groups which include, but are not limited to, people from minority ethnic backgrounds, people with disabilities, men wanting to teach in primary schools and people able to teach through the medium of Welsh in Wales. In accordance with current legislation, all workers who have contact with children are asked to complete a self-disclosure questionnaire confirming their physical and mental fitness to teach. If you have a disability, ITT providers will look at how they can make reasonable adjustments for your needs. By law, you are also subject to a criminal records check. It is vital that you disclose any criminal convictions when you submit your application. A criminal record will only normally count against you if it affects your suitability to teach. Failure to make an accurate disclosure could have serious consequences for your training and/or teaching. Situations do arise where trainees are asked to leave their ITT course because they have failed to disclose a criminal act from their past, so it is worth being totally upfront about any previous misdemeanours.

There is no doubt that job security and a decent pension is an important factor in any career decision. Pay in teaching has improved in recent years. Additional allowances may be paid to teachers who are considered excellent, and to those who take on management and other responsibilities. There are plenty of opportunities to progress. For up-to-date details of the pay-scale ladder please go to www.teachernet.gov.uk/pay, where an outline of the current pay scales is provided.

In addition to your salary you will receive a competitive and generous occupational pension package. In England, teachers may be eligible for help with housing costs through the government's key worker living initiative. You may also qualify for additional recruitment and retention incentives and benefits.

Hopefully this has provided you with a balanced view of teaching and you now have enough information to decide whether you would like to explore the issue further. The fact that many new teachers leave within the first three to five years of teaching indicates that teaching is certainly not a job for everyone. It also leads me to believe that these teachers did not carry out enough research before they entered the profession. Still interested? Then read on.

2 Is teaching the right job for you?

Arranging a school visit

It is all well and good to read up on the joys and pitfalls of being a teacher, but the only real way to discover whether teaching is for you is to get yourself into a school and find out. In our experience, there are three ways in which people usually do this, depending on their individual circumstances.

If you are in full-time employment, you will need to arrange to spend some time in a school, to observe and get the feel of what happens in classrooms, playgrounds and staffrooms today. This would ideally be a week in length, which would enable you to observe different age groups and see the full range of activities experienced by the children. If you are unable to take that much time out, a couple of days would certainly give you an introduction to primary school teaching.

If you are not in full-time employment, you may have the flexibility to volunteer in a school on a set day each week. Schools are usually very willing to accept volunteer help to hear children read, give support with groups, undertake administrative duties or lead extra-curricular activities such as after-school clubs. Many potential trainees decide to apply for posts as teaching assistants, on a full- or part-time basis, to learn as much as possible about education today. While spending time in a school you may be fortunate to work with or talk to a newly qualified teacher (NQT). An NQT represents a point along the continuum not too distant from where you are now. In other words, where you will be, should you be successful in your application to join an ITT programme. We would also advise that you talk to a range of teachers about the pros and cons of the job. Your school may even have a trainee with whom you can talk. He or she will certainly provide you with a different perspective from the one proffered by the TDA in its seductive glossy brochures. They will tell you how it really is. If you like what you see, and should you decide to take the process further and apply to an ITT programme, you will need to read the detailed guidance on what to look for in schools as outlined in Chapters 4 and 5.

Choosing to teach is a life-changing decision and should not be taken lightly. In addition to your school visits we would strongly advise you to carry out further primary research to ascertain whether you are really suited to the profession. The TDA website provides a wealth of information from which to make an informed decision about your possible future career. The website also provides video clips of teachers talking about life in the classroom and about their feelings towards teaching. In addition to this, it provides a list of frequently asked questions, all of which are highly relevant at this stage of your teaching journey. Some of the excellent advice is listed below, and further information can be accessed via the TDA website.

Open Schools Programme

If you are unable personally to arrange a visit with a local school you could do this through the Open Schools Programme which is sponsored and organized by the TDA but which only applies to schools in England. If you are interested in visiting an open school for a day you are advised to contact the TDA, although you do need to bear in mind that, owing to high demand for places, these visits are subject to availability. The programme gives you the chance to

- see at first-hand what it's like to be a teacher in today's schools
- find out if you like the school environment
- talk to teachers about their profession
- discuss topics such as managing children's behaviour.

Taster courses

If you are pretty sure you want to be a teacher, you might like to enrol on a three-day taster course designed to give you an in-depth view of teaching today and of the training options available. The following courses are run by the TDA and are available in England:

- courses designed for people from ethnic minority backgrounds
- courses designed for men who are interested in teaching in primary schools.

If these options do not meet your needs, it may be worth contacting your local authority to see if other courses are available locally.

Teacher advocate programme

The advocate programme allows you to speak to a teacher by phone or email. If you are interested in a career in teaching but haven't yet made the final decision, you can talk things over with an experienced teacher before you finally make up your mind. The teacher advocate programme will

- give you the opportunity fully to explore the issue with someone who will listen to you and who will more than likely mention things you had not thought of
- allow you to hear at first-hand what it's like to be a teacher today
- allow you to ask about the curriculum and related subject knowledge
- allow you to discuss issues that may be worrying you such as managing children's behaviour.

Face-to-face recruitment events

The TDA runs regular recruitment events where you can talk to experienced teachers, mentors, trainers, current trainees and NQTs about teaching. Alternatively, if you know of any ITT providers in your area, a simple phone call will determine when and where the next recruitment event will be held.

Impartial careers advice

If you are looking for impartial and objective advice then your local careers service can offer you advice about teaching. If you are a graduate considering a change of career, you can obtain impartial advice from the TDA's regional careers advisers. You might feel the assertion that the TDA will offer you impartial advice on the issue to be rather contradictory. After all, is it not in their interest to recruit new teachers? Of course it is, but we need to stress that this is not merely a 'numbers game'. It is more important for the organization to recruit enthusiastic, motivated and skilled people who will be highly committed to their training and teaching roles. Failure by the TDA to sift and sort people at this early stage would result in great financial expense in terms of wasted training costs, and would also be doing the trainees themselves a serious disservice. The TDA will give you the chance to:

- use a career-guidance specialist to help you explore teaching as a career
- get impartial advice about a career change to teaching
- find out about teacher training
- explore the best routes into teaching.

The student associate scheme

The 15-day student associate scheme has been designed for students interested in gaining classroom experience while still pursuing their studies. It gives them the chance to discover what teaching is like, work alongside experienced teachers and develop new skills. While they are on the scheme students are paid a bursary. The scheme is open to students registered on relevant HND, foundation degree, undergraduate degree and postgraduate programmes. The scheme gives you the chance to

- explore teaching as a career
- help raise the attainment and aspirations of young people in schools
- work alongside experienced teachers
- improve your CV by broadening your personal skills
- bring your subject knowledge into the classroom to support teaching
- do work aligned with the standards for qualified-teacher status
- receive a training bursary.

Another useful source of information in which you will find realistic teaching scenarios presented to you is the *Times Educational Supplement* (*TES*), and it is certainly worth obtaining copies of this on a fairly regular basis in order to keep up with contemporary issues. The 'New Appointments' section of the newspaper will be of particular relevance to you, as it covers a range of issues directly related to your role as a trainee and future NQT.

The purpose behind you seeking advice and/or visiting a school is for you to gain a 'warts and all' view of a typical school day and use this to make a decision as to whether to take the process further. However, if you'd like to understand what it's like to work with children, you are by no means limited to observing what goes on in a school. You could also volunteer to work in a youth club or sports club, or as a Scout or Guide leader. This will give you exactly the kind of awareness and experience to make your teacher-training application stand out from the crowd, should you decide to apply.

Those already working in schools

In recent years there has been an increase in the number of teacher trainees who have previously been employed in schools as teaching assistants or learning-support assistants (TAs and LSAs), cover supervisors and instructors. Many of these trainees used their time in schools to gain classroom experience before making their final decision to apply for an ITT course. ITT providers will certainly look favourably on those applicants who take it upon themselves to gain this level of experience before applying for their course. If you are interested in teaching and you have decided to take this route, make sure that you reflect on all you do. You could collect and annotate paperwork which may be useful for your portfolio of evidence when you begin your ITT course. Some providers will allow you to use recent evidence (usually no more than a year old) to meet some of the QTS standards which have been provided in Appendix 1 to help you.

The aim of this chapter has been twofold: to present you with a balanced view of teaching as a potential career; and to furnish you with a range of suggestions on how to find out more about life in a modern-day primary school. We hope that both these aims have been realized. If you are still interested in exploring teaching as a career then you need to read and inwardly digest the information provided in the next chapter which focuses on the nature of teacher training in general and on the different training routes available.

Choosing the right training provider

3

Having made the decision to teach, you now need to move on to the next stage of your journey: that of exploring your possible routes into teaching. This chapter will initially provide you with a detailed description of each of these routes before then going on to explore some of the factors that you need to consider when choosing a specific course.

Gaining QTS

Your teacher-training course, whichever one you decide to complete, will provide you with qualified teacher status (QTS), or its equivalent if you are training in Scotland or Northern Ireland. Depending on the course you take, you may also gain a BEd, a Postgraduate Certificate of Education (PGCE) or a Professional Graduate Certificate in Education (also a PGCE).

Choosing the right course

There are many different routes into teaching and hundreds of different initial ITT courses available in the UK. Choosing between them is a challenge in itself, but if you are going to find the course most suitable to your needs you need to be prepared to put in a lot of research. There are a number of things you need to think about before choosing an initial teacher-training course.

The subject and age group you intend to teach

ITT courses and programmes cover a variety of age-ranges within the primary school years. Courses are available which enable you to train to teach ages 3–8, 7–11 and 5–11 years. There are also some courses offering training in the middle years, namely 7–14 years. Many of these courses offer specialisms in areas such as early years, or in various curriculum subjects. The latter are often promoted as working towards leading a subject within the school after your NQT year.

Which ITT programme should you choose?

When choosing a teacher-training course it is important to consider and research all the possible pathways and opportunities available. It is essential to familiarize yourself with the structure of the course and the training opportunities offered. When selecting an appropriate ITT course it is vital that you give full consideration to your preferred way of learning, to your personal circumstances and to your past experiences. It is also important that, when finalizing your choice of provider and/or venue, you speak to past and present trainees about their experiences. Finally, it is essential that you choose a course which will offer you the best guidance and support during your training.

Each and every one of us has a unique set of personal, emotional, academic and social characteristics, and although it would be impossible to provide an ITT course which has been completely tailor-made to your individual requirements, there are specific courses that will prove to be more or less suitable to your needs. An overview of the various programmes is provided in Table 3.1.

Table 3.1 Summary of ITT courses available

Programme type	Course type	Abbreviation
Undergraduate	Bachelor of Education	BEd
	Bachelor of Arts/Science with QTS	BA/BSc with QTS
Postgraduate	Postgraduate Certificate of Education	PGCE
	School-centred initial teacher training	SCITT
Postgraduate	Graduate Teacher-Training Programme	GTTP
Employment-based	Registered Teacher Programme	RTP
Postgraduate assessment only routes	QTS only	QTS
Postgraduate overseas trained teachers	Overseas Trained-Teacher Programme	OTTP

Source: www.tda.gov.uk/Recruit/thetrainingprocess/typesofcourse.aspx

Baseline qualifications

Before you trawl through the range of information offered on the following ITT programmes, it is important to note that to train as a primary school teacher, you must achieve a standard equivalent to grade C in GCSE English, mathematics and science. For some BEd and BSc/BA with QTS courses, you may need A levels too. Make sure you check with the provider.

For all postgraduate courses (PGCE, SCITT, GTP) you will need a degree. To complete the Registered Teacher course, you need at least 240 Credit and Accumulation and Transfer scheme points (known as CAT points).

If you have qualifications obtained outside the UK, visit the National Academic Recognition Centre (NARIC) website www.naric.org.uk to find out whether they are of an equivalent level to UK GCSEs, A levels and degrees.

Each course is now described in more detail, but you will need to visit providers' websites or contact them directly to gain all the information you need.

Undergraduate courses

Bachelor of Education Degree course (BEd)

The Bachelor of Education Degree course (BEd) is a four-year honours degree course in education which will eventually provide you with QTS. These university-based BEd courses enable you to study for your degree and complete your initial teacher training at the same time.

How long does the course take?

Obtaining a BEd honours degree usually takes four years of full-time study, although if your personal circumstances require that you complete the course on a part-time basis, you can do so. If you do decide to study part-time, the course usually takes between four and six years to complete. If you have undergraduate credits from previous study you may be able to finish the course in two years.

Where can you do a BEd?

You can complete BEd degree courses at universities and colleges throughout the UK.

What qualifications do you need?

Although each university has its own specific course entry requirements, a minimum of two A levels or equivalent is usually required. You will need to contact your individual course providers to find out more details.

Is there any additional funding available?

The financial arrangements for these courses are the same as for all other undergraduate courses.

How do you apply?

Apply through the Universities and Colleges Admissions Service (UCAS): www.ucas.ac.uk/

When should you apply?

For most BEd courses starting in September or October, UCAS accepts applications between the preceding September and January. If you feel like taking a break before starting your training, rest assured that many universities are happy for a successful applicant to defer entry for a year.

What should you do next?

- Visit the UCAS website and search for BEd courses and find out more about the application process.
- Visit the NARIC website: www.naric.org.uk to find out whether your qualifications are of an equivalent level to UK GCSEs, A levels and an undergraduate degree.

BA/BSc with QTS

A BA or BSc with QTS is an honours degree that also incorporates teacher training. By taking a Bachelor of Arts (BA) or Bachelor of Science (BSc) degree with qualified teacher status (QTS), you can study for a degree and do your initial teacher training at the same time.

How long does a BA/BSc with QTS course take?

Courses generally take three or four years full-time or four to six years part-time.

Where can you do a BA/BSc with QTS course?

You can complete BA/BSc with QTS degree courses at universities and colleges throughout the UK.

What qualifications do you need?

Entry requirements vary according to the specific course, although a minimum of two A levels or equivalent is usually required. You do need to check with individual course providers for details.

Is there any additional funding available?

The financial arrangements for these courses are the same as for all other undergraduate courses.

How do you apply?

Apply through UCAS: www.ucas.ac.uk/

When should you apply?

For most BA/BSc with QTS courses starting in September or October, UCAS accepts applications between the preceding September and January. It is often also possible to apply to defer entry for a year.

Next steps

- Search for courses and find out more about the application process.
- Visit NARIC website: www.naric.org.uk and find out whether your qualifications are of an equivalent level to those required by UCAS, A levels and an undergraduate degree.

Postgraduate courses

Postgraduate Certificate in Education (PGCE)

Alternatively, you could gain a university degree in a subject of your choice and then gain your QTS by doing a one-year PGCE at a university. Training is usually carried out over a 40-week period excluding the summer holiday. A PGCE course focuses on the development of your teaching skills, and National Curriculum subjects.

How long does a PGCE take?

Courses generally last for one year full-time, or up to two years part-time.

Where can you do a PGCE?

PGCE courses are available at universities and colleges throughout the UK.

What qualifications do you need?

You must have a UK degree or a recognized equivalent qualification.

Is there any additional funding available?

Eligible trainees completing primary PGCE courses in England are entitled to receive a tax-free training bursary.

How do you apply?

The majority of PGCE applications are made through the Graduate Teacher Training Registry (GTTR) www.gttr.ac.uk. However, some ITT providers require that you approach them directly.

Next steps

- If you contact the Training and Development Agency (TDA) they will provide you with more detailed information about PGCE courses and other postgraduate routes into teaching, as well as regular news and updates from the ever-changing world of teaching and teacher training (www.tda.gov.uk).
- Visit the GTTR website (www.gttr.ac.uk).
- Search for PGCE course vacancies and course entry profiles, find out more about the application process and complete an application online.
- Visit the NARIC website: www.naric.org.uk. Find out whether your qualifications are of an equivalent level to UK GCSEs, A levels and an undergraduate degree.

School Centred Initial Teacher Training (SCITT)

There are a number of SCITT programmes which, like the university courses, also run over a 40-week period. These may be run in conjunction with local authorities or schools. If you are a graduate and want to complete your training in a school environment, consider this route. Taught by experienced teachers and advisers, and often tailored towards local teaching needs, all SCITT courses lead to qualified teacher status (QTS).

If you prefer to spend more time training in the classroom, putting theory into practice and gaining confidence through increased contact with the school environment, then a SCITT programme is a good option for you. A SCITT programme will still not give you as much time in school as the Graduate Teacher Programme, but it will give you the support of a group of fellow trainees meeting regularly for lectures.

How long does SCITT take?

SCITT training generally runs over a 40-week period from September to June. You need to be aware that some courses start earlier.

Where can you do SCITT?

There are consortia of schools and colleges running SCITT courses all over England. These groups provide all kinds of SCITT, covering primary and middle years. You need to be aware that there are currently no SCITTs running solely within Wales. However, some consortia run on the English-Welsh border, and may use Welsh schools as part of their programme. Some SCITT providers locate themselves in the lead school from the consortium while others base their headquarters in separate LA buildings.

What qualifications do you need?

You need a UK degree or a recognized equivalent qualification, as well as the required GCSEs.

Is there any additional funding available?

Eligible trainees completing SCITT courses in England are entitled to receive a tax-free training bursary. The precise amount depends on the subject and course start date.

How do you apply?

In most cases, you need to apply for SCITT courses through the Graduate Teacher Training Registry (GTTR), although some SCITT providers require direct applications. You need to visit the GTTR website for full details of available courses and methods of application.

When should you apply?

SCITT courses follow the academic year, so you start your training in August, September or October, depending on the provider. You generally need to apply through the GTTR or directly to the provider during the preceding academic year.

What you should do next

- Visit the GTTR website (www.gttr.ac.uk).
- Search for SCITT course vacancies, find out more about the application process and complete an application online.
- Visit the National Academic Recognition Centre (NARIC) website www.naric.org.uk to find out whether your overseas qualifications are of an equivalent level to UK GCSEs, A levels and an undergraduate degree.

Employment-based routes

Graduate Teacher Programme (GTP)

If you are not too concerned about obtaining the PGCE and are quite happy with QTS certification on its own, then you may like to think about applying for the Graduate Teacher Programme (GTP). The programme is delivered by a Designated Recommending Body (DRB) which could take the form of a single school, cluster of schools or a separate and distinct organization. The GTP is a programme of 'on-the-job' training, allowing graduates to qualify as teachers while they work. It is a good choice for mature people who want to change to a teaching career but who need to continue earning while they train. Once on the programme, your training will be tailored to your own individual needs and lead to QTS. While in your training school you will be employed as an unqualified teacher.

How long does the GTP take?

Training usually takes up to one school year, full-time, depending on your previous teaching experience. In certain cases, where the trainees have substantial relevant experience, you may be fast-tracked and can complete the course in as little as one term.

Where can you do the GTP?

You can complete the GTP in any English or Welsh state school, as long as they are prepared to employ you as an unqualified teacher for the duration of the programme, and they are working with a DRB. Independent schools can be involved in the GTP, but these applications would have to be self-funded. Pupil referral units cannot employ GTP trainees, nor have any involvement with the training. It is also not possible to train as a GT in a school that has had an Ofsted inspection and which has gone into special measures. It is important to bear in mind that some DRBs will allow you to choose and approach a school in which to train, whereas others will select a school for you.

What qualifications do you need?

You need qualifications at least equivalent to a UK degree, in addition to the baseline qualifications described at the beginning of the chapter.

Is there any financial support available?

Your school will pay you on an unqualified or qualified teacher's salary, which will be provided by the TDA in order to help meet your employment costs. The TDA also provides the school with a substantial grant towards your training. If the school does not receive this funding, there is also a self-funded option available, whereby the school will meet the costs of the GTP. To find out whether this option is available to you, you will need to enquire at your local GTP provider, known as an employment-based initial teacher training (EBITT) provider.

Registered Teacher Programme (RTP)

The Registered Teacher Programme (RTP) provides a blend of work-based teacher training and academic study, allowing non-graduates with some experience of higher education to complete their degree and qualify as a teacher at the same time. To take part, you first need to be working in a school as an unqualified teacher. This makes the RTP a good option for mature people who want to change to a teaching career but need to continue earning while they train.

Once on the programme your training will be tailored to your own individual needs and lead to QTS. You need to be aware that this is an incredibly demanding way to train as a teacher and is certainly not for the faint-hearted. It is usually recommended that you have significant experience of working with children before applying to take this route.

You can complete the RTP in any English school, as long as it is prepared to employ you as an unqualified teacher for the duration of the programme. Independent schools can be involved in the GTP, but these applications would have to be self-funded. Pupil referral units cannot employ RTP trainees, nor have any involvement with the training. Please note that the RTP is not currently available in Wales.

You must have completed the equivalent of two years (240 CAT points) of higher education. For example, you may have completed an HND, a DipHE or the first two years of a degree. The recognition of 240 CAT points is at the discretion of the RTP provider. Again, as with all teacher-training courses, you need the baseline qualifications in English and maths.

You must first find a school willing to employ you and support you through the programme. You then need to apply directly to your local EBITT provider, who will assess your application and establish what further training you would need to meet the standards for QTS. Some EBITT providers can help you find a post in a school – otherwise you can look for vacancies in the local and national press, as well as on local authority and recruitment websites.

You can apply to join the RTP at any time. Bear in mind, however, that it is a challenging programme, requiring substantial effort and commitment. The RTP is not as widely available as the Graduate Teacher Programme (GTP), and competition for places is high. You need to be sure that this programme is absolutely right for you before you apply.

Assessment-only route

If you already have a degree and substantial experience of working in a UK school as an instructor or unqualified teacher, or as a teacher in an independent school or Further Education institution, you may be able to qualify without undergoing any further teacher training.

The QTS-only option, or 'assessment only' as it is known, offers you an opportunity to demonstrate that you meet standards required to achieve QTS by compiling and submitting a portfolio of evidence of your abilities as a classroom teacher.

In addition to you providing this portfolio evidence, you will undergo a rigorous day-long assessment visit to your school. You need to be aware that the 'assessment only' process can take up to a year to complete, and that it can start and finish at any time.

The University of Gloucestershire administers this process for England, and the scheme is not available in Wales. If you are interested in submitting yourself for QTS assessment only, please contact the University of Gloucestershire School of Education directly and register with the TDA (www.glos.ac.uk/faculties/ehs/education/index.cfm).

Overseas Trained Teacher Programme (OTTP)

If you are qualified as a teacher overseas and outside the European Economic Area, you may be eligible to work in England as a temporary teacher without QTS for up to four years. This programme is currently available in England only.

Once you have found a teaching position in a school, the Overseas Trained Teacher Programme (OTTP) will provide you with your own individual training and assessment programme, which will ultimately lead to your qualification to teach in England permanently.

What qualifications do you need?

You must first be qualified as a teacher overseas and working as an unqualified teacher in a school in England. In addition, you will need a qualification equivalent to a UK degree as well as the baseline qualifications outlined earlier in the chapter.

How long does the OTTP take?

The length of the programme will depend on the extent of the additional training you need. However, the longest you can spend on the programme is one year full-time. If you feel your skills and experience are sufficient to meet all the QTS standards without further training, you may apply for QTS assessment only.

Is there any additional funding available?

If you need to undertake a programme of additional training, the TDA will make a contribution towards the cost of this training and towards the cost of your final assessment. Your school will continue to pay your salary.

How do you apply?

Once you have a teaching post and you have established that you have all the necessary qualifications, you should apply directly to an EBITT provider in your area. They will assess and approve your application, discussing your training needs with you as necessary. If resident in Wales, you may be eligible to join an employment-based route towards QTS.

When should you apply?

There are no deadlines for the OTTP although it is up to EBITT providers to establish start dates for programmes. The four-year rule for overseas trained teachers (OTTs) states that you can teach for up to four years before you have to gain QTS. The four years starts from the first day that you teach in a mainstream school in England, and includes any time out of service.

Next steps

- Visit the NARIC website to find out whether your qualifications are of an equivalent level to UK GCSEs, A levels and an undergraduate degree (www.naric.org.uk).
- If you qualified as a teacher in Scotland, Wales, Northern Ireland, another country in the EEA or Switzerland, you may be eligible for QTS without further assessment. You will need to contact the General Teaching Council for England (GTCE) to have your qualifications assessed.
- If schools are unable to fill a vacancy, they may advertise the post as an instructor role. You may be able to use this need as a bargaining tool to get them to act as a conduit for your teacher training.

ITT course content

It is not possible to provide a detailed outline of the course content of all ITT providers in the UK. Having said this, however, it is fair to say that there are common elements within all of the ITT programmes and you need to be fully aware of what you can expect when you embark on your course. This may sound pretty basic, but all teacher-training programmes have been designed to equip you with the skills and knowledge you will need to teach successfully. ITT programmes focus on a number of themes, all of which are linked to the QTS standards. Whatever programme you choose, your initial teacher training will involve you being shown how to

- gain a knowledge and understanding of the National Curriculum programmes of study
- set challenging learning objectives and plan effective lessons
- manage classes, promote good behaviour and minimize disruptions in your lessons
- assess children's progress and use this information to enable them all to learn
- use information and communication technology effectively
- become fully aware of the professional values expected of teachers, in their attitudes and behaviour towards children and colleagues.

Most trainee teachers (except for those on some employment-based or assessment-only routes) divide their time between a university, or other higher education institution, and a school, where they will undertake supervised teaching practice.

Assessment

Again, it is not possible to delve into the assessment criteria for every single ITT provider in the UK. Suffice it to say that the most common assessment tools are as follows:

- through lesson observations where your performance as a teacher will be assessed against the standards for QTS
- through the completion of a professional portfolio which requires you to provide evidence of having met all of the 33 QTS standards
- through the completion of a school practice/training folder which requires you to keep records of your times in each practice school and of the training provided in your ITT programme
- through the reflective process designed to move your professional practice on
- through the completion of assignments which link theory to practice.

Things to consider when making your choice

No two courses of initial teacher training are the same – largely because no two ITT providers are the same. Universities, colleges and schools all display varying characteristics, strengths and entry requirements, not to mention course content and structure.

- Bearing in mind that many postgraduates end up with serious debts after their courses finish, money might be an issue for you. If this is the case, it would probably be better to look for a locally based ITT programme which uses local schools. By doing this you then have the option of living at home and you will also be able to keep travel costs down. Unless you are lucky enough to have a university in your vicinity, the GTP and SCITT courses would probably be your best bet in this situation.
- If you would prefer to study a subject in depth before focusing on pedagogical issues, you would be advised to take a degree course and then enrol for a PGCE, SCITT or GTP course. If you would prefer to spend more time learning how to teach your subject then you may prefer to take the BEd degree course.
- It is important for you to have an understanding of your preferred learning style before you make an important decision such as this. If you are fully at ease in exploring the social, philosophical and theoretical side of teaching in detail you may prefer the BEd course. If you are a more kinaesthetic learner who learns quickly from practical experience you may prefer the SCITT or GTP option.
- Are you the sort of person who does not work particularly well under pressure? There is no doubt that the four-year BEd degree course is a more stress-free route through the teacher-training process compared with the one-year programme offered by the PGCE, SCITT and GTP courses, which usually involve a steeper learning curve for trainees.
- The willingness to make mistakes and to learn from them is a fundamental requirement of any good teacher. Having said this, some trainees are more comfortable with this principle than others. There is no doubt that a BEd course will afford you the most time and space to make your mistakes and to learn from them. Some BEd courses offer trainees up to four practices, which in essence represent four opportunities to start afresh and have another go at 'getting things right'. It is fair to say that the PGCE option offers fewer opportunities for trainees to 'start afresh'. Although most PGCE courses offer trainees two school practices, there are a number of courses that do ask their trainees to undergo three school placements. This is something you need to look into when applying for

your course. The GTP route offers you the most time in a single school. With the exception of a brief second practice, you will spend the whole of the academic year in one school. To this effect, therefore, if you make mistakes in the early stages of your practice you will either have to rectify these, or simply live with the situation for the complete academic year. This is certainly the course for the fast learners among you. Trainees who embark on a GTP course are contracted to the school for their training year and, as such, should be treated as bona fide members of staff. Many trainees are very happy about this and like to feel part of a real team, but you need to be aware that there can be a downside to this. You will be spending very little time with other trainees. Some GTP courses do bring trainees together either once a week or at certain times in the year, but most of your time will be spent with experienced teachers.

- The level of your life experience is also an important factor in helping you to decide upon your training route. The GTP is often a preferred route for graduates who have done something else before deciding to join the teaching profession. A GTP provider will go out of its way to help you identify and utilize the skills and qualities you have amassed during your previous working life to support your training and teaching. The fact that these skills and qualities are formally audited and given full credit at the beginning of the training year has attracted many older candidates to the GTP route. Although the GTP does provide opportunities to study the theoretical elements of teaching, the dominant learning tool for trainees is the time spent in the classroom.

Comparing training providers

It is absolutely vital, when you are deciding which type of ITT training you are going to embark upon, that you make a rational and informed decision. One of the things you could do to find out more about each of the ITT providers available to you is to visit the TDA's performance profiles website (www.tda.gove.uk) to search for and compare universities, colleges and schools.

This dedicated database will allow you to search through and define your ITT options and provide you with the performance profiles of the various ITT providers, thus making it easier to find providers which meet your specific requirements. The performance profiles database contains yearly data on all the universities, colleges or SCITT providers in England. Each ITT provider's record includes its contact details, the courses it offers and the characteristics of its trainees and details of their qualifications on entry to the course. These records also provide information, based on Ofsted inspection evidence, about the quality of providers' ITT courses, the proportion of their trainees gaining QTS on completion of their training, and how many enter a teaching job within six months of successfully completing the course.

In addition to enabling you to review and compare the detailed characteristics of ITT providers, the TDA performance profiles website also allows you to search for a provider or group of providers according to a range of different criteria, including:

- location
- subject specialism
- age group
- provider
- TDA quality category
- training route.

By using these criteria individually or together, you can generate a shortlist of ITT providers that match your preferences. You can then compare providers using their wesbite reports and narrow down your options further still.

If you want to train as a teacher in Wales

The TDA performance profiles cover ITT providers in England only. For information about providers of initial teacher training in Wales, you should visit the TDA website for Education and Learning Wales. You can also view information about provider performance in Wales on the Higher Education Funding Council for Wales website (www. hefcw.ac.uk). In addition, the Teacher Education and Training in Wales website (www.teachertrainingwales.org) provides details of all the initial teacher-training providers in Wales and the courses they run.

Funding and finances

Let's face it: this has got to be one of the major factors in deciding which ITT provider to choose, or indeed whether to embark on a teacher-training course in the first place. Unless you are fortunate to have sufficient funds to get you through the training period, it is highly likely that you will experience some debt during this period. Even if you embark on an employment-based route into teaching you are either highly likely to have run up debts at university, or if you have moved directly from paid employment on to the teacher-training course you are probably going to experience a significant drop in income.

Paying fees

For most teacher-training courses the university or college fees will be fully or partially paid for by the local authority (LA). It is therefore absolutely vital that you apply to your LA in plenty of time to see if you are eligible for your fees to be paid for you. It is important to note that once the LA has agreed to pay your fees, the agreement is binding and lasts for the whole time you are at university, even if you move to a different area.

Those postgraduate students who are thinking about applying for SCITT training courses should be aware that a number of them have started charging fees, although these may be partly paid by the LA.

Living expenses

Most undergraduates embarking on a four-year training course will probably take on holiday jobs to support themselves during this period. Even so, most of them will take out a low-interest loan from the Student Loan Company (www.slc.co.uk) which is a government-sponsored company set up to provide financial support for all students, irrespective of their courses. You need to be aware that this money does not have to be paid back until you start earning.

Additional financial advice

- You may be able to gain some financial assistance with childcare, travel and other course-related costs by contacting the DCSF through their website at www.dcsf.gov.uk
- Welsh trainees need to ask their providers about the Welsh Language Incentive.
- Visit the TDA website.

Part Two
MAKING THE MOST OF YOUR APPLICATION

Understanding your school visit 4

Understanding a school's ethos

Virtually all teacher-training providers will require you to have visited at least one school prior to you making your application. In Chapter 1 we discussed the importance of you gaining experience in schools, and stressed how unwise it would be for you to submit an application 'blind' without ever having determined whether life in a modern-day primary school is really for you. Time may be an issue for you, especially if you are busy working or have a hectic and demanding family life, but, in order to prepare yourself for the interview, you need to spend some time in different types of primary schools. Ideally you should visit a small rural school and a large urban school. Having said this, it is important to stress that merely spending a 'token' amount of time in a school is not enough on its own to prepare you for your interview, nor is it sufficient to provide you with the required background knowledge to inform fully your training or teaching. In short, you need to know what you are looking for. To this effect, therefore, we have provided structured guidance on how to use your visits in such a way as to prepare you for the interview and for your first school practice.

If you get the chance to visit more than one primary school you will notice that each school has a very different 'feel' about it. Every school has its own distinct culture and atmosphere which provides the visitor, and more importantly the children, staff and governors, with a strong signal as to its values and expectations. This is often referred to as the school's ethos, and it is based on a combined set of values and a joint vision, implicitly conveyed to the children. Although all schools have to follow the National Curriculum, they will have their own ways of planning how and when this happens, based on their beliefs and values about how children learn best. They will also have very different expectations of their children, for instance in the way that they are expected to behave towards each other and work together.

When you visit a school it is very important that you focus your attention on its ethos, and the way the school operates. Although you may understand the term as a generic principle, you may not yet be fully aware of what this actually means in practice. Bearing this in mind, therefore, we have provided you with a number of subheadings describing the areas you will need to explore during your visit. It will probably be worth making notes during your visit using these subheadings to focus your thoughts. You may think you will remember everything, but you won't. The experience will also prove to be invaluable when it comes to you gaining a full understanding of your practice schools, and of the schools you will work in during the course of your career.

How the school day and the curriculum are organized

The way in which a school organizes its teaching time can have significant effects upon the children's behaviour and the quality of the teaching and learning that takes place. The structure of the school day is dependent on how schools plan lesson times, break times and lunchtimes. In larger schools, these may be at different times according to age groups. Although all children will have some organized break in the morning, it is often only Key Stage 1 (KS1) children that have a planned break in the afternoon. Nursery and Reception classes, namely the Early Years Foundation Stage (EYFS) should have access to an outdoor environment throughout the day, and some KS1 classes may have similar opportunities. All EYFS classes experience six areas of learning, namely:

- communication, language and literacy
- problem-solving, reasoning and numeracy
- physical development
- creative development
- personal, social and emotional development
- knowledge and understanding of the world.

KS1 and KS2 children follow the National Curriculum, which currently consists of ten subjects and religious education. However, this is currently under review, and will change in 2011. Despite having a common curriculum, there is, and always will be, huge variation in the way that schools organize the teaching of this. At present, in the most formal of schools, all subjects are timetabled separately across the week, often with literacy and numeracy occurring in the morning when, theoretically, most children have better concentration. Some schools ability-group their children into 'sets' for core subjects, while others favour mixed-ability teaching at all times. Some schools have fairly formal timetabled mornings, with more creative, fluid afternoon sessions where subjects merge and a more topic-based approach is followed. Sometimes whole blocks of specific subjects are timetabled during a particular week, allowing the best use of resources and teacher time. For example, children may complete a whole technology project in a week so that the design, making and evaluation process is continuous; there is less 'clearing up' and 'setting up', and children get more fully involved with making their products.

In many schools, barriers between some individual subjects are blurred. In these cases, there may be many cross-curricular links, so that subjects are taught together. For example, history and literacy may be combined so that the skills of writing are taught while learning about Ancient Egypt. In the most creative of schools, curriculum subjects are combined in many different ways, sometimes in a highly innovative format. Role-play, puppets, visiting experts and interactive computer experiences may be used to help children learn.

Some questions you might like to focus on are detailed below.

- How is the curriculum organized? Distinct subjects? Cross-curricular themes?
- How are different abilities catered for?
- How do morning and afternoon sessions differ?
- How does the Early Years Foundation Stage curriculum differ from that in KS1?
- How does Key Stage 1 differ from KS2?
- How does the curriculum differ from that which you experienced in your own education?

The structure of lessons

Many of the lessons you observe in a primary classroom, apart from those in the Foundation Stage, will involve three main parts: an introduction; a main part where children undertake activity in order to learn; and a plenary where the teacher uses a variety of methods to summarize the learning that has taken place. The first stage, or introduction, often takes place with the children sitting on a carpet in KS1, or at their tables in KS2, with the teacher introducing the learning objectives or learning intentions for the session. Often the teacher will describe how the lesson links to previous learning, or will ask the children if they can remember what they learned yesterday. They will then often take the opportunity to introduce new vocabulary and terminology. In the main part of the lesson, children will undertake activities that help them learn, while the teacher either works with a group or assesses and guides individual children. During the plenary, children are often given the chance to demonstrate their learning, while the teacher may ask them to evaluate what they have done. You may see the teacher stop the class to give them a 'brain-break', when they undertake a short physical activity to re-energize them. You may also see children moving around to access water bottles or even snacks, so that hunger and thirst do not hinder learning.

In Foundation Stage classrooms, that is in Nursery and Reception classes, you may not see this sort of structure. However, there will be times when the teacher addresses all children for various purposes, and these may happen at different times of the day. Much of these children's learning is play-based, where teachers and other adults may set up activities or let children choose what they want to do, following their interests and strengths.

Behaviour management

Schools will vary significantly in the way that they manage the behaviour of the children. However, in many classrooms there will be a list of 'rules' or 'responsibilities' which has been drawn up at the beginning of the year, involving the children to some degree. Many will have lists of rewards and sanctions which the class teacher will use to ensure the children follow the rules. Most good teachers will employ a significant amount of praise in any lesson to encourage children to behave. There is certainly much emphasis in today's classrooms on creating a positive learning environment in which children feel able to contribute, ask questions and feel good about themselves. Many schools have investigated how children learn best, based on recent scientific knowledge about how our brains work. It is also worth looking out for methods teachers use to make children think about their behaviour, to make choices and take responsibility for their actions. There may be children in the school who exhibit particularly challenging behaviour. They may have individual behaviour plans and there may be an additional member of staff employed to work with them.

You could focus on the following questions:

- How do teachers use positive language to manage behaviour?
- How do teachers convey what they expect in terms of behaviour?
- What sanctions are used in the school?

- How important is consistency in the classroom and across the whole school?
- How is this aspect of education different from your own?

Extra-curricular activities

Many teachers and support staff devote a great deal of time to clubs at lunchtimes and after school. These can involve sport, arts and crafts, games, nature, drama, gardening, chess and many others. Many schools are heavily involved in competitive sport and will devote time and energy to matches and training. Others participate fully in musical activities, where instrument tuition, choirs and orchestras are all laid on. There is a huge variety of people involved in running these, including teachers, support staff, parents, volunteers and specially employed instructors and tutors. Some smaller schools join forces or involve local secondary schools to provide a wider range of activities.

You could use the questions laid out below to help your enquiry into this aspect of school life.

- What extra-curricular activities and school trips do the school provide, and how are they provided?
- How do these extra-curricular activities and trips help to improve the quality of the relationships between teachers and children?

Assemblies

Sociologists have argued strongly that schools can be seen as microcosms of society and that the social conditions prevalent within the workplace and society in general are often deliberately replicated within the school environment. The extent to which this should be the case can be debated at a later date, but what is important for you to realize is that one of the functions of the school is to prepare its children for life in the outside world. Nowhere is this preparation more obvious than in school assemblies. These provide excellent opportunities to engage in themes such as inclusion, friendship, courage and diversity. They are key times when the whole school or groups from the school come together to provide strong messages about the school's ethos, and for school leaders to share their beliefs and values. In church schools these are times to participate in shared religious beliefs.

Assemblies may involve the whole school, Key Stages or classes on different days. Some schools hold assemblies at the beginning of the day, some before break and some at the end of the day. There are often opportunities for parents to be involved, either through sharing in a particular theme or celebrating children's achievements.

Some questions to be considered are

- What are assemblies used for?
- Who leads them?
- What do children learn from assemblies?
- How do assemblies reflect the school's ethos?

Quality of classroom and corridor displays

Positive messages can be transmitted to children through the medium of effective classroom and corridor display. Bearing in mind that we know the school's ethos is a set of values, attitudes and knowledge-frames which are embodied in the organization and processes of schooling, you will appreciate that the classroom and corridors are the perfect places in which to do this. It is now the role of the support staff in schools to organize and produce displays of children's work, but these will often still be designed by the teachers. The purpose of displaying children's work is to let them know it is valued by the teacher; inform parents about children's achievements; help children think and improve on first designs and to appreciate the work of others. Technological developments such as digital photography and film are extending teachers' work here, with children's efforts being captured on a daily basis. Here are some starting-points for thinking about the displays you will see:

- How is the ethos of the school reflected in its displays of children's work?
- What **expectations** are being transmitted through the medium of classroom/corridor display?
- How do classroom/corridor displays encourage a positive attitude towards work?
- How do classroom/corridor displays encourage a positive attitude towards the school rules?
- How do classroom/corridor displays encourage respect for others?

Making the most of your lesson observations 5

It is sometimes difficult to see what a good teacher is doing well in a classroom. They use techniques and skills which they have learned and perfected over time. The authors use a lot of video observation when working with trainees, using clips from Teachers TV (www.teachers.tv) which they learn to evaluate, in preparation for watching clips of their own teaching. However, they invariably find it easier (and more enjoyable!) to describe why poorer lessons fail, rather than why good lessons go well. Good teachers simply make it look easy! To this end, we have formulated two observation proformas which you might want to use when observing in schools. The first focuses on behaviour management and the second looks at the teaching and learning process. Good behaviour management is obviously vital, but is not enough on its own! We have both seen trainees spend so much time enforcing rules and giving sanctions that there is little or no time for learning. Equally, if the lesson is instantly engaging and continues to stimulate and interest all abilities, there will be less need for behaviour-management strategies to be deployed. However, you may want to focus on either one or the other to help you see what is going on.

These proformas do not involve making judgements about how good or bad a lesson was, they merely get you to describe how teachers do things. It is worth looking at each aspect of the teacher's work individually. In this way, you will start to see what teachers actually do, and why they do it.

PROFORMA 1: BEHAVIOUR MANAGEMENT	
DATE: **SUBJECT:**	
Things to look for:	**What I noticed:**
START OF THE LESSON	
How does the teacher get the class ready to learn at the beginning of the lesson?	
How does the teacher engage the attention of children who are not ready?	
How does the teacher ensure only one child is talking at a time?	
How does the teacher use praise with the children?	
How does the teacher use his/her voice?	
How does the teacher use body language to convey messages?	
MAIN PART OF THE LESSON	
How does the teacher keep an eye on everyone?	
How does the teacher gain attention of the whole class?	
How does the teacher convey his/her expectations? Has he/she used any sanctions?	
END OF THE LESSON	
How does the teacher ensure everything is cleared up and tidied away?	
How are the children dismissed from the room?	

PROFORMA 2: LEARNING AND TEACHING	
DATE: **SUBJECT:**	
Things to look for:	**What I noticed:**
START OF THE LESSON	
How does the teacher start the lesson?	
How do the children know what they are going to be learning?	
How does the teacher use the interactive whiteboard?	
What types of question does the teacher ask?	
How does the teacher 'model' or set expectations?	
How does the teacher organize group/ individual activities?	
MAIN PART OF THE LESSON	
How does the teacher keep an eye on everyone?	
What questions does the teacher ask?	
How does the teacher provide feedback to individuals?	
How are different ability groups catered for?	
How does the teacher monitor progress of all the children?	
How are children encouraged to evaluate their own work?	
END OF THE LESSON	
How does the teacher reinforce the learning?	
How do children evaluate their own learning?	

Having carried out your observations, it is important that you start to collate and synthesize your findings in order to come up with a set of generalized learning points. By doing this you will be in a better position to share your new-found expertise, and articulate these experiences during your teacher-training interview. Some examples are shown below.

Lesson observation summary focusing on: effective behaviour management

- My observations taught me that it is imperative for teachers to set out their rules, routines, expectations and sanctions when they first meet their class and to then revisit these constantly. This practice was most effective when teachers provided the rationale behind their rules, routines and sanctions, and involved the children in writing them in the first place. I now understand my need to make my expectations clear to children from the very outset.
- I noted that the most effective learning environments occurred in classes where the teachers obviously knew a lot about the backgrounds of the children within their charge. These teachers showed a high level of respect for their children, even in situations where they had to impose sanctions. All the other children saw this as being 'fair'. I will make it my business to research the background of my children before I start teaching my class, and to establish relationships with the parents as quickly as possible.
- It was interesting to note that the best-behaved classes were those in which a 'can do' culture had been engendered by the teacher. In many lessons, good behaviour was achieved through the teacher's use of positive and supportive language when responding to children's contributions in class discussions and question-answer sessions. I was also interested to note how good teachers made meaningful use of praise as a behaviour-management tool. They used phrases such as 'I like the way you're sitting nicely Ryan ...' to get everyone to do this.
- What absolutely 'shouted out' at me while I was carrying out these observations, was how children responded so positively to teachers who demonstrated 'teacher warmth' and who showed a sense of humour in their lessons. I will endeavour to keep my sense of humour even if things go badly in my lessons.
- Children behaved best in lessons where their teachers adopted a *consistent* approach when issuing sanctions and when admonishing their classes. In other words, in situations where teachers 'said what they meant' and 'meant what they said', children knew exactly where they stood and behaved accordingly. I will make sure that I am robust in following up on issues that arise in my classroom.
- What dawned on me very early on in my observation experience, was how important 'teacher presence' is in gaining effective control over classes. I witnessed numerous lessons where the teacher used effective body language, eye contact and voice tone to dominate their teaching space. I will make it my business to observe good teachers at work in the classroom and to try to develop my teacher presence.

Lesson observation summary focusing on: effective child learning

- The best lessons occurred when teachers provided the children with a variety of activities and tasks. Some teachers overtly set up activities that catered for the various learning styles of their children. By doing this the teachers were able to engage fully the visual, auditory and kinaesthetic learners within their classes. I will find out how the children in my classes learn best.
- I discovered that children learn best when the teacher has made the learning objectives transparent and when these are revisited on a regular basis during the lesson. I will make sure that I ask my children whether they understand the purpose of each lesson.
- I found out that children also learned best when their teachers issued clear sequential instructions. I will write my instructions down and show these to my class teacher before I start teaching my lessons.
- The most positive learning environments were created where children felt comfortable in making mistakes and where it was 'OK to be wrong'. I will try to build up a climate of trust in my classroom. By doing this, my children will realize that making mistakes is just part of the learning process.
- The most effective lessons were those that had an effective 'introduction', 'core' and 'plenary'. I will make sure that my lessons are well structured and that I provide that initial 'hook' which will get my children 'on board'.
- I was really impressed by the way in which some teachers managed to involve every child in their discussions and/or question-answer sessions. In these classes no child was 'marginalized'. I will try to ask a question of every child during the course of each lesson.
- In some lessons, children were given the opportunity to assess their own work as well as the work of their peers. I felt that this increased the ownership of their learning and kept the youngsters on task. I will try to get children to evaluate their own work and to feed back their findings to the rest of the class.
- In some lessons I witnessed an excellent use of ICT. Some teachers made good use of PowerPoint to cater for the visual learners in their classes, while others made superb use of the interactive whiteboard fully to involve their children. Other teachers used ICT to run quizzes in the 'starter' phase of their lessons. I now realize the importance becoming ICT proficient.

If you use your pre-interview school visits in this way, you will feel more confident when completing your personal statement and you will also be more likely to perform well at interview. In short, you will have made your school visit work for you.

6 Preparing to make your application

The application form is a conduit through which you are expected to provide evidence of your social and communication skills, and to demonstrate how you can organize your information in a clear and accessible manner. It is therefore vital that you take every opportunity to get the spelling and grammar on your application form thoroughly checked. You are also strongly advised to make a copy of your application form and take it along to the interview. This will provide you with a last-minute reminder of the issues that may be brought up by the interview panel.

Having spoken with a number of current and potential trainees about the application process, we have arrived at the conclusion that the personal statement is the section of the application form that most candidates find difficult to complete. Many current trainees felt that with hindsight they did not fully do themselves justice in being able to demonstrate their skills, experience and enthusiasm for teaching young people, and for teaching their subject. This chapter attempts to offer advice on how to do so.

Although it is very important that you use the application process to display your individuality and uniqueness as a person, it is important that you keep within specific parameters. To help you to do this we have provided a number of questions for you to consider when completing your personal statement:

- Why do you want to be a teacher? Who or what has influenced your decision to apply to join the profession?
- Why do you think you will enjoy working with children? What previous experiences of working with children can you bring to your training and to the profession in general?
- What relevant skills and personal qualities are you able to bring to the teaching profession?
- How have you developed your subject knowledge and how will you use your expertise to enthuse, motivate and inform your children?

- How have your experiences in schools or other educational environments informed your view about teaching?
- What else can you offer the profession in terms of extra-curricular interests?

It is important that you give your personal statement a great deal of thought and that you complete this as comprehensively as you are able. Although we have provided some exemplar responses overleaf, it is vital that you emphasize your own individual experiences and that your statement does not appear to be too formulaic. Remember that training places are limited, so try to make your personal statement as original and appealing as possible.

We would also strongly endorse the advice proffered by the Training and Development Agency (TDA) which warns applicants not to over-claim. ITT providers are highly likely to explore the statements you make in more depth. If you are found to have made a false claim it will almost certainly seriously jeopardize your chances of getting on to your course. We have both been witness to situations where trainees have given false information and have been asked to leave the course. It is always best to be 'up front' when making your application.

Let us now explore these questions in more detail.

Why do you want to be a teacher? Who or what has influenced your decision to apply to join the profession?

The responses to this set of questions will provide the opening sentences to your statement and, as such, it is very important that you get it right. In the introductory chapter we explored some of the reasons why people wanted to become teachers. If there was a specific time when you decided to become a teacher, then you need to describe how you came to this realization. The TDA once ran an inspirational campaign entitled 'No one forgets a good teacher!' This recruiting message was conveyed extensively on cinema and television screens and on billboards across the country, and was a resounding recruiting success. If you were inspired by particular teachers when you were at school, then you could briefly describe the effect of these teachers on your decision to apply for a teacher-training course. Examples of possible openers from the TDA website include:

- 'What attracts me to teaching is …'
- 'I am interested in teaching because …'
- 'Teaching appeals to me as a career because …'

The next question for you to consider when writing your personal statement requires you to relate your experiences of working with young people to your application to become a teacher.

Why do you think you will enjoy working with children? What previous experiences of working with children can you bring to your training and to the profession in general?

You need to link the skills used in these situations to your potential role in the classroom. Three exemplar statements are provided below.

Example A

While I was at university I carried out some voluntary work in a local primary school. One of my reasons for doing this was to see whether teaching really was for me, and to also get an idea of what it might feel like to be an adult in a classroom. I also intended to use this experience to ascertain whether my personality was more suited to teaching primary rather than secondary age children. While at the school, I was allocated the role of 'Right to Read Tutor'. This role involved me assisting children who were experiencing difficulties with reading and required me to work on a one-to-one basis with these youngsters over a five-week period. I found the whole experience extremely rewarding and thoroughly enjoyed my time in the school. To further support this experience I spent some time in a secondary school helping teachers to run the Young Enterprise Scheme. This scheme gave me the opportunity to work with Year 9 children on English-related issues over a five-week period. At the end of the five weeks I was asked to stand up in assembly and present these youngsters with their certificates. Although I was extremely nervous at the time, both experiences proved to be thoroughly enjoyable and helped me to make the decision to apply to teach.

Example B

In order to find out about my suitability for teaching, I became a Teaching Assistant (TA) in my local primary school. While carrying out this role I learned a great deal about children with special needs and was pleased to discover that I was able to strike up good working relationships with even the most challenging of children. As my role required me to work with individual children across the curriculum, I was fortunate enough to observe a whole range of teaching and learning styles. I was also able to witness teachers carrying out their classroom-management strategies with varying degrees of success. In making this decision to apply to train as a teacher, I am doing so having gained a full and realistic view of classroom life.

Example C

Although I have had no formal teaching experience, I feel that my work with the Scouts over the past five years has stood me in good stead making this application. In addition to helping to run the regular weekly meetings and activities, I have also been involved in helping to organize and run summer camps in the Lake District and the Norfolk Broads. My role involved me working on a one-to-one basis with young people on their 'personal targets' and helping groups of youngsters to 'set up camp' and organize the competitive activities that took place during our stay at the site. I would certainly welcome the opportunity to use my organizational and interpersonal skills in a classroom situation.

The next question for you to consider when completing your personal statement relates to the skills and qualities you have amassed throughout your lifetime. According to the TDA website there are many qualities that can be attributed to good teachers. They suggest that a good teacher should demonstrate:

- an ability to relate to young people, good interpersonal and listening skills
- the capacity to be alert, creative, imaginative, energetic and enthusiastic
- an ability to be adaptable and versatile
- a sense of responsibility and reliability
- good time-management and organizational skills
- resilience, motivation, tenacity
- a desire for self-development.

The question set out below requires you to focus on the attributes that match your own strengths and to identify a specific time when you have demonstrated those qualities. Three example answers are provided.

What relevant skills and personal qualities are you able to bring to the teaching profession?

Example A

I am a good team worker and have particularly demonstrated this skill playing football for my local team over the last six years. I was appointed team captain and have represented our side in local, county and national competitions. I have recently trained as a children's football coach and now run an under-10 side that competes in the Sunday morning league. I am keen to develop my coaching skills further and to use these to help young people to improve their performance. I believe these skills and qualities to be fully transferable to a classroom situation, and am hopeful of being given the opportunity to show what I can do.

Example B

After leaving university in 2007, I spent a year in Zambia as a voluntary aid worker for the Save the Children charity organization. During my stay in the country I lived in a small village just north of Lusaka. Some of my time was spent helping the villagers and other aid workers to build wells in the villages in the area. At other times I helped experienced teachers in the teaching of English in the local primary school. Not only did this extremely rewarding experience allow me to get my own life into perspective, but it stimulated my desire to give something back to the world. Teaching would be my way of doing this.

Example C

On leaving university I accepted a post with a local insurance company. Within a year I was appointed section supervisor with a responsibility for ten members of staff. On getting the job I was told by my own supervisor that, among my other skills and qualities, it was the high quality of my organizational and interpersonal skills that had specifically led to me landing the job. I feel that these two qualities are of vital importance both to the training year and to the teaching profession in general.

There is no doubt that good subject knowledge is high on the TDA's list of priorities for trainee teachers. When writing your personal statement, you need to make sure that you include information about your subject strengths and how you have continued to develop these. It is also worth reflecting on your weaker areas and doing some reading/research into these to demonstrate your willingness to gain the necessary knowledge. Below are two exemplar responses to the following key question.

How have you developed your subject knowledge and how will you use your expertise to enthuse, motivate and inform your children?

Example A

I have always had a passion for environmental science and since completing my degree in this have been an active member of a local wildlife group, contributing regularly to education sessions for children and families. I have recently led activities with Guides and Scout groups on pond-dipping. I have also become a member of a local 'green' group, and have read widely on a variety of current environmental issues. An area of curriculum weakness of mine is music, and I have made a conscious effort to listen to a wider variety of performers and attend a series of local concerts.

Example B

Throughout my academic career, history has always been a subject that has excited and challenged me. In order to meet the demands of my degree course I have developed such skills as analytical thinking, persuasive writing and the ability to communicate orally. Taking history to degree level has greatly improved my research skills as well as my ability to interpret primary and secondary sources. I used these skills to gain a first-class honours grade for my dissertation which focused on the role of women during the First World War. While I was in my second year at university I was fortunate to accompany a Year 6 class to the town's castle and its immediate surrounds. This experience provided me with real insight into how the teachers used the children's previous knowledge and experience to help them explore and interpret the rationale behind the construction of a number of local historical buildings and monuments. This has made me really keen to develop my own pedagogic skills in such a way as to inspire my children and engender a similar love of history within them.

How have your experiences in schools or other educational environments informed your view about teaching?

You will remember the advice given to you at the beginning of this chapter about your need to visit a range of schools and to take full advantage of your experiences. This is now your chance to reflect upon your school experiences and show how perceptive and astute you have been during your school visits. You should identify and comment on particular aspects of your experience and demonstrate how these affected the teaching and learning processes. Some examples include:

- the way the curriculum was taught
- the individual teacher's personality or behaviour-management techniques
- the way the teacher assessed work and gave feedback to children
- how the teacher worked with other adults in the classroom.

Again, two exemplar statements are provided for your perusal:

Example A

During the last year of my degree course, I had the opportunity to visit a local primary school one afternoon a week. I have been amazed at the creativeness of the teachers there, who have managed to plan a stimulating way of delivering the National Curriculum through real-life examples and scenarios. I have seen children make enormous progress in literacy and numeracy through being truly inspired by the enthusiasm of the staff. I have observed the way that the school invites parents to share in their children's learning, and would like nothing more than to be part of this too.

I established good relationships with teachers and children alike in my short time there, and feel now that teaching is definitely the career for me.

Example B

I have worked as a TA in a primary school for the last five years. I have learned an enormous amount about behaviour management, and particularly the importance of building good relationships with children, valuing them as individuals and understanding their background and motivation. Last year I helped set up a nurture group in school to help develop a group of children's social skills. This has been a fascinating learning journey for all concerned, and I have learned to measure success in small steps, to chart each individual's progress and to share success widely in the school community. This has inspired me to take the giant leap to train as a teacher – to make an even bigger difference to children in the future.

The final question requires you to think beyond your immediate remit as a trainee. When selecting applicants, all ITT providers will look beyond the training period to the time when most of you will be employed in schools on a full-time basis. Through the medium of your personal statement, they will seek to find out what additional contributions you will be able to make to the schools in which you will eventually be employed.

What else can you offer the profession in addition to your own specialist subject?

Here, you should focus on other skills you have that would be of benefit to a school. These could be

- language skills, including modern foreign languages or community languages such as Urdu or Punjabi
- your interests, such as photography, ICT, sport, drama or music
- a training experience or management skills you have gained in other employment.

Three exemplar statements are provided below:

Example A

As a native Bengali speaker I can use my linguistic skills and cultural understanding to offer support to children in the school for whom English is a second language.

Example B

I was a junior professional at the local football club, and would love to coach this sport. I would be keen to set up football teams and to help teams participate in local tournaments.

Example C

I have a passion for gardening, and have recently completed the Royal Horticultural General Certificate course. I would love to set up a gardening club in a school, and am fully committed to the eco-schools agenda. I would be interested in helping children to grow their own fruits and vegetables and to cook healthy meals with them.

By now you will have realized the importance of the application form and, in particular, the personal statement in the 'sifting and sorting' process carried out by ITT providers. Having completed your application form to the best of your ability, you are strongly advised to find a friendly teacher in a local school and ask them to read it through before you eventually send it off. Chapter 8 offers guidance on how to prepare for your interview, and perform well on the big day.

Part Three
PREPARING FOR THE SELECTION DAY AND BEYOND

Completing the
selection tasks

7

Bearing in mind that the reputation of ITT providers depends very much on having a small 'drop-out rate', they will do absolutely everything they can to select appropriate candidates for their courses. Before being accepted on an initial teacher-training programme, you will probably be asked to attend an interview which will usually take place over a full day, but which may take as little as one hour. When you receive the call to attend an interview, it is very important that you read the letter and information sheets very carefully. A number of ITT providers require you to carry out a pre-interview task, so be careful not to miss this among the paperwork. You may be asked to read a book or an educational article of your choice and then be prepared to discuss this on the day. If you want to be fully prepared for the interview, make sure you use the information gained from your reading to *identify the potential implications of this material* on your teaching. For example, if you have read an article on managing challenging classes from the *Times Educational Supplement* (*TES*), then you need to identify and describe some of the things you would need to do in order to manage your classes effectively. If you have chosen to read up on different learning styles, then you need to know how you might put this to good use in the classroom. Being able to identify implications from your own practice, or from observations of others, is a vital reflective skill and one which you need to be able to use throughout your career.

Alternatively, you may be required to carry out a piece of small-scale school-based research, which will then be discussed at your interview. It is important that you identify the implications of your findings for your potential practice as a teacher. You could, for example, be asked to find out how a school tackles the subject of bullying. Any interview panel would be extremely impressed if you were able to identify examples of observed good practice, and if you then went on to show them how you would use or adapt these ideas for your own teaching purposes.

There are some ITT providers that will require you to sit tests and carry out tasks on the day of the interview. This process could take the form of a comprehension exercise, which would require you to respond articulately to an educational article or extract presented to you on the day; a presentation; a group task; an ICT activity or other subject knowledge-based tests.

There are also some ITT providers who require potential trainees to work with children for a part of the interview day. Potential trainees may be asked to prepare a presentation for a group of children or to read them a story. Personnel from the ITT provider, teaching staff, teaching assistants and children may be asked to provide feedback about your performance. Some of the criteria they may be looking for include:

- making eye contact with the children
- positive body language
- appropriate use of voice
- gaining children's attention
- scanning techniques
- ability to give clear instructions
- good relationships with children
- ability to think on your feet
- presence
- management of children's behaviour
- appropriate use of resources.

It is important to make your presentation/activity/story as dynamic and memorable as possible – include audio and visual input if you can, and try to get the children actively involved in discussions and/or question-answer sessions. You may also consider bringing relevant resources into your session. We have seen a number of potential trainees use items such as puppets, masks and small world play equipment to stimulate discussion or to help tell stories.

This can be quite a daunting experience for you, especially if you have only made a few visits to a school since you left school at the age of 16 or 18. However, just thank your lucky stars that you are not being made to teach a complete lesson, as is the case with many trainees who attend selection days at the end of their training. Now, that really **is** stressful!

It is also highly possible that this 'sifting and sorting' process will continue to occur **after** your interview has taken place. Some ITT providers require you to participate in further recruitment exercises which may include any of the following:

- a group task, discussion or presentation
- a further individual interview and/or
- written tests in a variety of subjects.

The interview

8

Then there is the interview itself. The format of the interview can vary greatly between ITT providers. Your interview could take place on a one-to-one basis, or it could be a panel interview. In some interview scenarios the process will be extremely formal, with you sitting opposite a small panel of lecturers and/or senior staff. Alternatively, your interview may be far more informal and relaxed than this. We have found that in situations where interviews take place in schools, rather than in Higher Educational Institutions (HEIs), candidates are far more likely to encounter a more informal approach to the process. Whichever stance members of the panel adopt, you need to remember that they are trying to get to know you, and to ascertain whether their ITT programme and, indeed, whether teaching in general, is really for you. With this in mind, it is important that you try to answer questions fully, so that the panel get to know you properly on a personal and professional basis. It is fair to say that you need to take every opportunity to elaborate on the information provided in your personal statement, and that your responses should be sufficiently detailed to have answered the question, but you need to be very careful not to waffle. This is why it is important that you rehearse your responses beforehand.

There is absolutely no doubt that you will be asked about your experience of working with children, about your commitment to teaching, and about your relevant knowledge and skills. The providers are also looking for applicants to show evidence of their full commitment to the profession. A proficiency in, and an enthusiasm for, teaching is obviously an important element of your application. However, providers are looking for far more than this. They require you to provide evidence to show that you have demonstrated a full commitment to the social and academic well-being of children, and are far more likely to offer a place to someone who can discuss concrete examples of situations where this has occurred. One thing interviewers will tend to focus on during the interview process is how much passion and enthusiasm the candidate displays when talking about their experiences of working with young children. My advice to you therefore, would be to talk enthusiastically about your experiences, but to be very careful not to lose focus. The panel will require you to offer specific examples of the relevant experiences you have had before attending the interview. Below is a list of prompts to help you prepare, although this is by no means exhaustive:

- working with parents
- helping children to resolve conflicts
- managing challenging children
- supporting the learning of children
- assessing children
- organizing or helping with trips
- running clubs.

During your interview, the panel will be looking to see whether you fully understand the qualities required to be an effective teacher, and whether in fact you possess some or all of these. In preparation for your interview, you would be well advised to think about the ways in which you can show that you do have what it takes to join the profession. As you will see overleaf, the qualities required to be an effective teacher have been provided in diagrammatic form in Figure 8.1. To do so in list form would give the impression that these qualities are hierarchical in value. You need to show that you recognize the value of all these qualities, and that you understand how they interact with each other to produce the successful teacher.

As your interviewers will be looking for you to demonstrate those qualities displayed in Figure 8.1, you need to tailor your answers and contributions to reflect these when responding to their questions.

An additional prompt list has been offered below:

- a commitment to, and understanding of primary education and of the role of the teacher
- good personal, intellectual and communication skills
- a positive attitude towards children and working with children
- an enthusiasm for, and understanding of curriculum subjects and teaching in general
- the ability to express yourself in clear and accurate spoken English.

The panel will not only be listening very carefully to the quality of your responses, but they will also be keeping a close watch on **how** you deliver these responses and whether you possess the potential to command the attention of children in a classroom. To this effect, therefore, you are advised to take the following guidance on board:

Good mental and physical health

A keen interest in the development of children as well as in NC subjects

An interest in child development and a caring nature

An ability to cope well under pressure and to be well organized

Qualities needed to make an effective teacher

Patience, tolerance and perseverance

Sensitivity and empathy

An ability to think creatively and laterally

Ability to collaborate with adults and children irrespective of their background, class and ability levels

Various forms of intelligence – emotional intelligence highly desirable

Self-confidence and assertiveness

Figure 8.1 Qualities needed to make an effective teacher

It is up to you to use the time allocated to you during your interview to convince the interview panel that you understand the need for, and that you possess, many of these qualities.

- ensure that you are dressed appropriately for the interview
- make a confident but not arrogant entrance into the interview room. Shake the hands of each member of the interview panel and make good eye contact with them
- ensure that you adopt a confident body posture; that you hold your head up and that you keep your shoulders back. Make eye contact with the interviewers when they ask you a question
- no matter how nervous you are, try to look as self-assured as possible
- do not mumble – speak clearly, assertively and with authority. Take a few seconds to think over the question and collect your thoughts before you start to answer
- under no circumstances should you fabricate or exaggerate your experiences. As is the case with making false claims on your application form, if you are found out, you will be refused entry onto the course.

It is absolutely vital that you fully prepare and rehearse for your interview, as a failure to do so will result in a great deal of frustration on your part when you realize that you have not done yourself full justice on the day. You need to think very carefully about the types of questions you are likely to be asked by the interview panel. If you know any current trainees or NQTs who could advise you on the interview process, you need to sit down and go through the potential questions with them. Whereas it is virtually impossible to identify every question you may be asked by an interview panel, experience allows us to suggest a number of fairly predictable areas of enquiry. To help you to prepare for your interview, we have provided you with a list of possible questions.

Q: What made you want to become a teacher?

Q: What qualities do you think make a good teacher?

Q: What experience do you have of working with children and how could you utilize this in the classroom?

Q: What skills and qualities could you bring to the teaching profession?

Q: How could you motivate and inspire children who do not share your love of a particular subject?

Q: Can you identify one topic within any subject area that you feel might be difficult for children to understand? How could you deliver this topic in an accessible manner?

Q: How do you feel about the National Curriculum? Is it help or hindrance to children's progress?

Q: Describe how the contents of an article/book/extract you have read recently might impact upon your professional practice.

Q: How might you deal with children who constantly talk over you while you are trying to deliver your lesson?

Q: How will you ensure that you show respect and include children of all backgrounds in your teaching?

Q: What is the contribution parents can make to their child's education?

The TDA have produced an excellent interactive interview for you to practise with. This can be found at: www.tda.gov.uk/Recruit/thetrainingprocess/makingyourapplication/theinteractiveinterview.aspx

Preparing for your training course 9

Assuming that you have been successful in your interview, you now need to consider what you can do to prepare for your training course, which will commence about six months after you have received your acceptance letter. There are two main areas you can usefully pursue, namely visiting a variety of schools and doing some worthwhile reading. However, both of these need to be really focused in order to be useful. In this chapter, we have attempted to provide some structure for and guidelines to these activities.

The first area to look at is that of visiting schools. In an ideal world it would be profitable to arrange further visits to as many different types of schools as possible. It would be useful to observe and comment on similarities and differences between contrasting schools. If you can, compare large and small; urban and rural; traditional and innovative, and even those in different authorities. Try to observe as many classes as possible. At no other time in your career will you be afforded as many opportunities to observe a range of teachers at work. Having said this, you need to undergo this process with tact and sensitivity. No matter how competent or experienced a teacher is, he or she is still likely to experience a degree of self-consciousness and discomfort when being observed, even if it is only by an inexperienced pre-course trainee. Try to put the teacher's mind at ease by making positive comments about the wall displays or about the children and their achievements. Make it clear that you want to learn from her and that you are not there to judge her performance. It really is worth keeping notes of all the things that might prove useful to you later on in your career. Always thank teachers for the good ideas that you have gained from watching their lessons. If you are able to go one step further by taking on some temporary work as a Learning Support Assistant or cover supervisor, then take every opportunity to do so. This experience, especially if it is supported by considered reflection, will be invaluable to your training and to your future teaching career.

The second area of preparation you can undertake is to become confident in each and every area of the curriculum. In order to be an effective primary teacher, it is essential that you have the subject knowledge to be able to teach all subjects of the National Curriculum to the relevant age-range of children for which you are training. As part of Janet's role in a SCITT programme, she has the responsibility for training mentors working with trainee teachers in school. One of the largest areas of work she has been involved with recently is helping them to develop their trainee's subject knowledge for teaching (SKfT) based on the work of Fay Turner and colleagues (Rowland et al., 2008). This team of researchers has devised a four-step model to help mentors and trainees understand what they have to know in terms of subject knowledge across the whole curriculum. They identify the overt subject knowledge; the pedagogy needed to transform that knowledge so that children can learn; the curriculum knowledge and then the ability to use all these in the classroom to respond to children's ideas and misconceptions. From our experience of observing trainees, it is only when they have mastered all of these, that they are fully confident and competent to teach classes independently. The best lessons are those in which the trainee has high levels in each of these areas of SKfT.

You can be developing your knowledge and understanding in the first three areas once you have been accepted on an ITT course. A useful exercise is for you to carry out an audit of your subject knowledge using the National Curriculum. This will help you with all these areas. Work your way through the programmes of study for Key Stage 2, and identify where you have strengths and weaknesses. For example, you may note that your knowledge of biological science is good, but you would need to read up on particular aspects of 'physical processes' such as types of force or vibration and sound. To improve your overt subject knowledge, you could then use children's books, textbooks or the internet to read widely and improve your confidence in these areas. It is worth keeping notes of all you research – this will be very useful for you when you undertake your first teaching practice.

If you are volunteering or working in a school, you can start to examine the pedagogy – the ways teachers help children to learn these concepts. For example, teachers may have a very good knowledge of the work of Florence Nightingale, but to help children learn about her work, they would need to understand the pedagogy also, which they would demonstrate by:

- Using a timeline to help children understand chronology – when things happened in relation to their own lives

- Setting this work in a context, so children know what else was going on in the world at this time in history
- Using key historical vocabulary to enrich the children's learning
- Devising activities that help children understand Florence Nightingale's work – helping them ask and answer questions; discovering information; demonstrating their knowledge
- Enabling each child, regardless of ability, to understand the key concepts

Your observations could focus on how the teacher helps the children learn the subject matter. You could also take time in school to learn more about the curriculum. By spending some time in each class, from Reception to Year 6, you could improve your knowledge of how the children's understanding builds up, and how teachers' expectations change through the school.

In addition to providing you with a useful insight into your various roles as a potential teacher, we hope we have gone some way to whetting your appetite for further reading on pedagogical issues such as this. With this in mind, we have provided you with a list of publications which you might want to read before you embark on your teacher-training course.

Preparatory reading list

Clarke, S. (2001) *Unlocking Formative Assessment*, London: Hodder & Stoughton

Eyres, I. (2007) *English for Primary and Early Years: Developing Subject Knowledge*, London: Sage

Hayes, D. (1996) *Foundations of Primary Teaching*, London: David Fulton

Haylock, D. (2005) *Mathematics Explained for Primary Teachers*, London: Sage

Howe, A., Davies, D., McMahon, K. and Towler, L. (2005) *Science 5–11, A Guide for Teachers*, London: David Fulton

Riley, J. (2007*) Language and Literacy 3–7: Creative Approaches to Teaching*, London: Paul Chapman

Rogers, B. (1998) *You Know the Fair Rule*, London: Pitman

Smith, A. (1996) *Accelerated Learning in the Classroom*, Stafford: Network Educational Press

Whalley, M. (2001) *Involving Parents in their Children's Learning*, London: Paul Chapman

Wilson, A. (2005) *Creativity in Primary Education*, Exeter: Learning Matters

Wragg, E. (1994) *An Introduction to Classroom Observation*, London: Routledge

In addition to this you can download schemes of work from the Qualifications and Curriculum Authority (QCA) by logging on to the following web address: www.qca.org.uk/nq/

Earlier in the chapter we advised you to acquaint yourself with current educational issues as a means of preparing for your interview. We strongly suggest that you continue to do this by making a point of reading the quality press. The *Times Educational Supplement* is published every Friday and is the main source of educational news. Other newspapers such as the *Guardian* (Tuesday), *The Times* (Monday), the *Daily Telegraph* (Wednesday) and the *Independent* (Thursday) have educational supplements which are all well worth reading.

One of the things that you are bound to notice while you are carrying out these initial reading tasks is the substantial use of acronyms and educational jargon included in the text. Education, like every other profession, has its own specialized language, and as trainees it is important that you become accustomed to using this in your everyday professional life. To this effect, therefore, we have dedicated the next chapter to exploring some of the key educational terms that you are likely to encounter during your training period.

Part Four
GETTING TO GRIPS
WITH THE JARGON

10 Understanding key educational terms and issues

Understanding key educational terms and issues

Anybody starting work in a new business or entering a new profession is highly likely to undergo induction training that has been designed to familiarize new entrants with the norms, values and culture of that organization. An integral part of this culture is the language used to communicate efficiently with people across the various components of the organization. In short, if they are to function efficiently in these organizational roles they need to learn the jargon and understand the issues associated with the terminology. Teaching is no exception to this. From the very early stages of your teacher training you will be bombarded with a code of educational shorthand that you will simply have to get to grips with if you want to function efficiently within the world of education. This can be a bewildering experience for trainees and even newly qualified teachers.

You need to know that we have been highly selective in our choice of the key terms presented to you in this chapter, and that we have only focused on the terminology that you are likely to encounter in your training. You will also note that alongside the description of some of these key terms we have added brief guidance notes to help you to apply this new information to your professional scenarios.

Attention-deficit Disorder (ADD)

Attention-deficit Disorder is similar to ADHD (see below) but without the hyperactive tendency. ADD is more common in females than in males and is often overlooked because of the absence of the disruptive behaviour that is usually associated with ADHD and which affects the learning of other children in the class. Children suffering from ADD are often extremely quiet and insular, and have a tendency to withdraw from other children. As is the case with ADHD, children find it difficult to focus in lessons, and this lack of concentration tends to have a negative effect upon their academic performance. However, unlike ADHD children, who are quite robust in demonstrating their failure, ADD children often fail quietly.

Attention-deficit Hyperactivity Disorder (ADHD)

Attention-deficit Hyperactivity Disorder has been recognized as a medical condition as well as a behavioural disorder. According to Leibling and Prior (2005) ADHD affects around 2 per cent of the population and is more prevalent within males than females. There is a substantial body of research that suggests the condition is genetic, and you as teachers will probably find that it has affected more than one member of the same family. ADHD results from an imbalance of dopamine and noradrenaline, both of which are required to transmit messages between brain cells. Symptoms of ADHD include:

- lack of attention – short attention spans which result in children failing to grasp the main thrust of the lesson even though they are not without academic ability
- hyperactivity – inability to sit still in one place for very long
- impulsiveness – children act spontaneously and fail to think about the consequences of their actions.

Bearing in mind the antisocial nature of this disorder, it is not surprising that children with ADHD are often rejected by their peers and find it difficult to make friends. This sense of isolation can often lead to a lack of self-esteem, depression and anxiety, and can lead to the child self-harming or taking drugs. In an effort to feel wanted, many of these youngsters get in with the wrong crowd and often become involved in acts of delinquency and crime. At home, their behaviour is often seen as destructive; their hyperactivity means that they usually need less sleep than other members of the family and often keeps them awake at night. In addition, youngsters with ADHD can also have other disorders such as Autistic Spectrum Disorder.

Research carried out in the USA suggests that most children with ADHD underachieve, especially when it comes to reading and writing. As teachers, it is very important for us to be fully aware of this condition and not to label children as unintelligent and/or deliberately disruptive. To support you in your dealings with ADHD children you may find some of the strategies listed below useful in keeping them on task in your lessons. Obviously, some of these will only apply to older primary children, and you will have to seek further advice within the school in which you are training:

- Be explicit in describing the exact type of behaviour you expect from the child.

- Be explicit in outlining the consequences of any negative behaviour to the child.
- Help the child to recognize the danger signals and plan ahead. Discuss the scenarios in which the ADHD child is likely to lose control and rehearse some possible solutions with him or her.
- Explain the benefits of the children behaving appropriately and support good behaviour with rewards.
- Reinforce the child's success and effort.
- Ensure the child is sitting close to you in the classroom.

Advanced Skills Teacher (AST)

An Advanced Skills Teacher post provides an excellent opportunity for a high-quality teacher who wants to progress up the career and salary ladder but who doesn't want to relinquish his or her work in the classroom. Many ASTs have led core-subject teams, been part of senior leadership teams or have had responsibility for initiatives in their schools such as ITT. They can be appointed by individual schools or by the LA. The fundamental tenet behind the appointment of ASTs is that they should be responsible for cascading good practice to teachers in schools other than their own. This work is known as outreach work. It is highly likely that you will come across ASTs either in a mentoring role and/or at the training sessions organized and run by your ITT provider. You would be well advised to cultivate relationships with these teachers because they can often be an important source of advice on subject-related or generic matters.

Anger management

Anger-management sessions are designed to help children handle their anger in such a way as to minimize the negative effects on themselves, their families, their peers and the school in general. The idea behind this approach is to take a child's anger, turn it into a positive force, and then use it to engender self-control and raise achievement.

It would be extremely unrealistic to expect you as a trainee teacher to be able to take prime responsibility for the anger management of the more challenging children in your classes. In fact, to assume this responsibility would be extremely unwise and dangerous. Having said this, providing you liaise with the class teacher, there are things you can do to support a child with anger-management issues. One of the first things you need to do is to make yourself aware of some of the things that could make a child angry. If you try to change a child's behaviour without understanding the reasons behind her actions and reactions, you could badly escalate the situation. In attempting to ascertain these reasons, you need to be aware that there are boundaries which you as a trainee should not cross. To this effect, therefore, you are always advised to seek guidance from experienced colleagues and run your ideas past those who have a more intimate knowledge of the child concerned. It is essential that you treat every child as an individual and that you spend time ascertaining each one's needs. Here are some of the common reasons for children's anger:

- family break-up – divorce, separation
- physical or sexual abuse
- lack of self-esteem
- frustration at not being able to understand the work
- frustration at not being provided with the opportunity to show what they can do (teacher not catering for child's learning style)
- feeling deprived or victimized by other children or by teachers
- physiological and/or hormonal changes causing mood changes.

To support you further in your dealings with children who experience anger-management issues we have provided some brief guidance notes:

- Offer the child opportunities to talk and let him know that it is normal for people to experience anger. When you are doing this, you need to try to show empathy for the child's situation.
- Model the type of behaviour you wish to engender within the child, rather than demonstrate your own anger by retaliating.
- Help the child to find goals and positive objectives in life.
- Help to raise the child's self-esteem by getting him to produce a 'can do' list of things he is good at, both in and out of school.
- Make the child aware of the impact of his anger on others.
- Make it absolutely clear that hurting people or damaging other people's property is simply not acceptable behaviour.
- Help the child to identify the cause of his anger, and to recognize and deal with the trigger-points that occur along the way.
- Help the child to release his energy in a more constructive way, for example sport, yoga and so on.
- Find a way of getting the child to redefine his anger so that it becomes a positive force and a catalyst for success.

Autistic Spectrum Disorders (ASDs)

Autistic Spectrum Disorders, of which Asperger's Syndrome and autism are examples, are brain-based disabilities that affect language, communication and/or information-gathering. These disorders mainly affect the male population. Because their social and communication skills are particularly challenging, people with ASD often experience difficulties in understanding how to behave. Their use of language is often pedantic and they may have a tendency to take things literally. It is important to note that some, but not all, ASD children experience learning difficulties. In order to prepare you for teaching ASD children, we have provided you with some broad characteristics of the disorder below. However, it is vital that you do not jump to conclusions about the child without consulting the teacher with whom you are working.

ASD children find it extremely difficult to:

- interpret the meanings behind normal everyday conversations
- know what to say
- have a meaningful conversation
- form social relationships with adults and their peers
- show empathy or concern for other people
- behave appropriately
- participate in group activities
- hide their feelings
- use their imagination
- accept novelty or changes to their routines.

Assertive discipline

This form of behaviour management is based on the presumption that teachers have the right to determine the behavioural rules in the classroom, and that they also have the right to expect their children to comply with these. Assertive discipline in schools was developed in the 1970s by Lee and Marlene Canter, in the belief that poor behaviour in classrooms should not be allowed to impinge on the learning of others. Schools may adopt some of the principles of this approach, along with ideas from other strategies. The main characteristics of assertive discipline are laid out below:

- Teachers should take responsibility for outlining their expectations, and for establishing the rules that define acceptable and unacceptable behaviour.
- Teachers should teach the child to follow their rules.

- Teachers should make the children aware of the sanctions that might be imposed if they do not follow the rules.
- Teachers should show consistency in the imposition of their sanctions.
- Teachers should expect participation and support from parents and colleagues.
- Children should expect to have a teacher who sets limits and who motivates and respects them.
- Teachers should give children opportunities to manage their own behaviour.

Assertive discipline requires teachers to be assertive and confident in applying their learning rules. If the teachers are tentative, unclear and inconsistent in their approach to classroom management, then children can often become anxious, confused and even hostile. Teachers who practise assertive discipline provide feedback to children about their positive behaviour and usually employ their own reward system. Bearing in mind that at this stage of your development many of you will not yet be confident and assertive teachers, you need to remember that teaching is a journey and not a destination. Making yourself aware of the characteristics of assertive discipline and practising being confident and assertive will go some way to improving your behaviour-management technique. One way you can do this it to carry out some reciprocal peer observations using the proforma provided in Chapter 5 and using the observation notes to feed back to your colleagues. This really is a case of practice making perfect.

Assessment

There are three ways to assess children's work:

- **Criterion referencing** assesses achievement in absolute terms and simply measures whether a child knows X or can do Y. It can be used to asses a child is in relation to the National Curriculum levels.
- **Norm referencing** assesses a child's achievement in relation to a group, rather than in absolute terms: for example is this child in the top 10 per cent of the assessed population group?
- **Ipsative** assessments measure the progress of a child: i.e. what he or she can do now in relation to what he or she could do before.

You will also have to get to grips with the terms 'summative' and 'formative' assessment. In the past, the assessment of children's work tended to be mainly summative (i.e. assessment **of** learning). Traditionally, parents were furnished with annual reports of their children's academic performances, and this brief overview provided them with a snapshot of their progress. In 1998 the Assessment Reform Group concluded that there was a fundamental need for teachers to use formative assessment (assessment **for** learning) in their lessons as a means of raising achievement. Further details of each kind of assessment are given below.

Summative assessment is a snapshot of each child's achievements. This can take a number of forms: as an annual or termly report, or in the form of the publicized Standard Attainment Test (SAT) results. Summative assessment is often used to keep parents informed of their children's progress. It is also a useful tool for informing the teachers of the progress and achievements of children new to the school. It provides an indication of the children's strengths as well as of the weaknesses and gaps in their knowledge and understanding.

Formative assessment of a child's work is usually carried out by the teacher on an ongoing basis throughout a course or project and is used to aid learning. Formative assessment might also involve the learner and/or his or her peers in providing feedback on work, and is not necessarily used for grading purposes. There is further information on this area in Chapter 29.

Bloom's taxonomy of the cognitive domain

Benjamin Bloom published his taxonomy in 1956. This taxonomy is a commonly used hierarchy of thinking skills and learning abilities, starting with the easiest skills and working through to the most cognitively challenging 'high-order' skills. These skills are set out in order of difficulty below.

1   **Knowledge** – requires the children to simply recall information and facts from memory. This could take the form of biographical material about a famous person, historical dates, capital cities of the world, and so on. Questions testing this basic skill would begin with: *inform me, describe, tell me, list, define, who, when, where* and so on.

2   **Comprehension** – requires the children to show their understanding of the meaning of a specific element of knowledge by explaining things in their own words. It also requires them to be able to understand the implications of this knowledge. This is normally assessed by asking questions beginning with: *explain how or why, tell me in your own words, compare x with y, discuss*, and so on.

3   **Application** – requires the children to apply a concept to a novel situation. This could take the form of asking them to solve a new problem with existing knowledge. Activities testing application would start with: *apply*, *solve*, *experiment*, *discover* and so on.

4   **Analysis** – requires the children to dissect a complete entity or problem into parts and recognize the patterns of parts that make up a totality. This could take the form of troubleshooting a specific situation; or ascertaining where things started to go awry in any given system. Activities that test analysis would begin with: *analyse, find, identify, sort out, deconstruct* and so on.

5   **Synthesis** – requires the children to construct something new from existing parts. For example, this skill is tested in technology, where children are required to design and produce something that achieves specific objectives, or when they have to rearrange what already exists in order to satisfy new needs. This skill is normally assessed by asking the child to: *synthesize, create, design, invent, and devise.* Questions such as 'What if . . .?' might be used.

6   **Evaluation** – requires children to weigh up the evidence presented to them and make decisions about the value of something, for example from a range of possibilities select the most suitable solution. This skill is normally assessed by asking children to: *evaluate, judge, compare, select,* and so on.

So why is knowledge of Bloom's Taxonomy so important to the teacher? The fundamental reason why you need to understand this learning framework is so that you can differentiate the work you give your children. There is evidence to suggest that the most able children will benefit from work planned from the upper levels, and this may be a good way of extending them without moving them up through curriculum levels. It is also important that your teaching does not remain within the first level, even for the least-able children, as there is no point in them simply remembering facts without some degree of understanding or being able to apply them. You can also use Bloom's Taxonomy to differentiate the questions you ask your children in class and group sessions. By targeting questions at the right level to specific children within a class, you will be able to afford them the opportunity to show what they understand, and ultimately what they can do. This will also mean that the least-able children are asked questions within their comfort zone, and the most able are challenged and do not switch off. It would be useful to observe an experienced teacher doing this, although it is hard to spot if you do not know the abilities of the children! An intimate knowledge of Bloom's Taxonomy is therefore an essential ingredient of personalized learning.

Brain structure

It is important for you as trainees and future teachers to have a basic knowledge of the structure of the brain and how it affects learning. The simplest explanation is that offered by the triune model (see Figure 10.1).

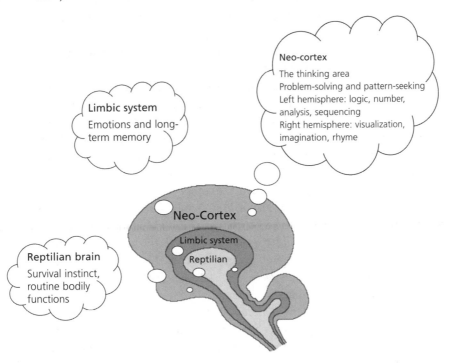

Neo-cortex

The thinking area
Problem-solving and pattern-seeking
Left hemisphere: logic, number, analysis, sequencing
Right hemisphere: visualization, imagination, rhyme

Limbic system

Emotions and long-term memory

Reptilian brain

Survival instinct, routine bodily functions

Neo-Cortex
Limbic system
Reptilian

Figure 10.1 The structure of the brain (adapted from Dixie, 2005, p. 71)

The reptilian brain is the area at the base of the brain which controls our survival instincts when we are put under threat. When a child feels insecure, unsafe or threatened, this part of the brain dominates and sets up mechanisms designed to protect the individual. In situations such as these, the child may become so frightened that he or she simply cannot answer questions and clams up. This often happens in tables, tests or mental arithmetic sessions, and also happens to adults in interview situations! Alternatively, the child may become hostile or will simply turn tail and run. This is why the reptilian brain is often called the 'fight or flight' part of the brain. Making sure that you deal with child misdemeanours in an assertive rather than an aggressive manner will provide the child with an opportunity to calm down and also maintain his dignity in front of his peers. As this part of the brain also controls our basic bodily functions, it is also important to make sure the classroom is well ventilated and that children have access to plenty of water. It will also cause a child problems if he is tired, hungry or upset from a situation at home. This part of the brain acts rather like a handbrake in a car. It is said that 80 per cent of learning problems are caused by stress-related issues (Shaw and Hawes, 1998) so, if the needs of the reptilian brain have not been met, the handbrake will remain on and learning will not take place.

The limbic system can be found in the middle of the brain and is thought to control our emotions and long-term memory. Bearing in mind that positive emotions produce endorphins that help to speed up learning, it is in the child's best interests that you create a positive 'can do' culture within your classroom, and that you provide her with an opportunity to have some fun in your lessons. It also helps this part of the brain to draw on the child's emotions and memories by relating the learning to her own experience.

The neo-cortex is positioned at the top of the brain and is thought to be the 'thinking' or 'cognitive' area, where problem-solving and pattern-seeking occur. The neo-cortex itself is divided into two distinct hemispheres, each with a different learning function. The left hemisphere is thought to be the verbal and analytical side of the brain that controls facts, language and logic, whereas the right hemisphere focuses on the non-verbal, creative and intuitive element of our personalities, as well as controlling our movement. Different children may have more strengths on one side or the other, which is worth bearing in mind so that you can set appropriate work that will both cater for, and challenge, their **learning styles**.

Catchment area

Some areas of the country have school catchment areas. The catchment area is a geographical area that provides a feeder population for the school. Even though a family may live within the catchment area, the parents will still have to apply to the school for a place for their child. All parents may apply to a school outside their own catchment area, but their success in gaining a place for their children will depend upon a number of factors, such as the capacity of the school and whether they have siblings already there.

Career Entry and Development Profile

This is a document that enables you to review your strengths and goals for the future towards the end of your training and through your first year of teaching.

Differentiation

This is defined by Ofsted as '. . . the matching of work to the differing capabilities of individuals or groups of children in order to extend their learning.'

When you start to teach, it is difficult to judge the abilities and skills of a particular year group, let alone the needs of the most and least able. However, through assessing what all children know, understand and can do, you will gradually begin to learn how to extend the most able children in each subject, and how to support the learning of those with special needs. This has to be considered in your planning, and in your interactions with children throughout the lesson. Differentiation can be achieved in a variety of ways, such as by

- planning different tasks
- questioning – this is where teachers ask questions at a level appropriate to the ability of the child (see Bloom's Taxonomy)
- use of an additional adult to support or extend a group
- setting different targets within a common task
- providing more structure within a task to support the least able
- providing more open-ended tasks for the more able children.

Dyslexia

Dyslexia is a complex learning disability that mainly affects spelling and reading, although the disorder can also cause children to experience difficulties with writing and number work. Many people go through their lives without having had their dyslexia diagnosed, but they have simply devised their own coping strategies to get by. Many children, previously labelled as 'less able' or 'lazy', are extremely relieved to be diagnosed as having dyslexia. The important thing for us to note as teachers is that dyslexia is not linked to intelligence. Children with dyslexia get very confused with the sequences of numbers or letters that make up a date or that spell a word. Some features to note are

- **Speech:** Children with dyslexia are often able to demonstrate their intelligence orally with some success, but this is not matched by their use of the written word. Poor spelling is often a big issue with these children.

- **Late development:** Many youngsters with dyslexia are slow to learn speech, tell the time, tie shoelaces, and may get confused between right and left. They may also experience difficulties with their motor skills such as catching, throwing, skipping and jumping, all of which require some degree of sequential thought.
- **Reading:** Children with dyslexia really struggle with reading, often complaining of letters being jumbled up. They often get their letters mixed up when reading text, for example mistaking 'b's for 'd's and vice versa. Children with dyslexia will often do everything they can to avoid reading in class, especially out loud.
- **Concentration and memory:** Children with dyslexia often have difficulty in concentrating for long periods of time. It is also true to say that their short-term memory may be poorer than their peers. As a result of this, they may be very slow to complete the tasks you set them in class and may have to give up without finishing.
- **Achievement:** In most but not every case, children with dyslexia will underachieve.

Bearing in mind the large number of children with dyslexia in our schools, it seems apposite to offer some guidance on how to get the best out of these children.

- Make sure that you 'headline' the main points of the lesson before you start teaching them. Constantly check their understanding of what you have told them. Provide a verbal summary of what you have taught them, before then asking what they have understood and not understood. Make sure that you praise, reinforce and correct where necessary.
- Do not refer to people with dyslexia as 'dyslexics'. Using this term creates a master-label for a child that does not do justice to the qualities and characteristics of the whole person.
- Provide regular breaks for these children, especially if the activities require them to concentrate for long periods of time.
- Integrate these children with the rest of the class wherever possible.
- Take full account of their condition when marking their work, and do everything you can to promote a positive attitude towards their learning and self-image.
- Use mind-maps with these children when you can.
- Make sure that you constantly repeat your instructions, but do so in a patient manner.
- Adopt a positive attitude towards dyslexia. Avoid using terms such as 'overcoming', 'disability', 'handicap' or 'drawback'.

- Always write down the homework and other instructions you might expect other children in the class to remember.
- Provide them with scaffolding when helping them to organize their work.
- Never ask them to read out loud.
- Always liaise with the special needs coordinator (SENCO) about these children.

Dyspraxia

Dyspraxia is a coordination disorder which manifests itself in clumsiness and disorganization of thoughts and movements. Children with this disorder may have difficulty with their fine motor skills, thus making it difficult to produce legible handwriting. They may also find it difficult to use a computer mouse in a coordinated and effective manner. Their gross motor skills may also be affected and they may experience difficulties in PE lessons where they are required to catch a ball or maintain their balance. Children with dyspraxia also have problems with sequencing movements and thoughts, so would find it difficult to imitate other people's actions. Getting organized for school is likely to be a problem. As the case with dyslexia, it is thought that the signals from the brain are not correctly received by the parts of the body that need to act on the signals.

English as an additional language (EAL)

This is the teaching of English to speakers of other languages. During your training you will learn how to support these children. Often EAL children arrive mid-term and without warning, so teachers have to be prepared for this challenge.

Foundation-stage profile

The foundation-stage profile is a way of summing up each child's progress and learning needs at the end of the foundation stage. For most children, this is at the end of the reception year in primary school.

General Teaching Council (GTC)

The General Teaching Council was founded in 2000 as an independent non-profit-making professional body for qualified teachers. It has been afforded statutory powers to advise the Secretary of State for Education on matters relating to teaching and learning. You are now required by law to join the GTC, irrespective of whether you work in a maintained, non-maintained, special school or pupil referral unit. As a trainee you do not have to join the GTC, but when you gain QTS your name will be put onto the teaching register and you will soon be asked to make arrangements to pay the annual fee.

Governors and governing bodies

Governing bodies exist for all schools. The role of the board of governors is to ensure high educational standards, take general responsibility for the conduct of the school's affairs, and oversee the budget, the curriculum and the appointment of personnel to the school. The governing body also has a responsibility to respond to Ofsted reports. The board of governors consists of the head teacher, local authority appointees, support-staff representatives, elected parents, elected teachers and members of the local community. It is the duty of the governors to read all the relevant material, to keep up to date with current educational practice and to meet on a regular basis.

Individual education plan (IEP)

An IEP is used for all children in special schools and for children with specific learning difficulties in mainstream schools. It typically covers language, literacy, mathematics, behaviour and social skills. An IEP provides information that indicates:

- what type of help has been given to the child
- how often the child receives this help
- who has provided this support
- what the current targets are for the child
- how and when the child's progress will be monitored
- what help the parents are giving their child
- what the next moves are for providing additional support for the child.

Key Stages

A Key Stage is a stage of the state education system in the UK setting out the educational knowledge and understanding expected of students at various ages. The stages are as follows:

- Early Years Foundation Stage (EYFS): birth – 5 years

- Key Stage 1: Years 1–2 (5–7 years old)
- Key Stage 2: Years 3–6 (7–11 years old)
- Key Stage 3: Years 7–9 (11–14 years old)
- Key Stage 4: Years 10–11 (14–16 years old). The exams at the end of this key stage are typically of the GCSE level.
- Key Stage 5 (more commonly referred to as Sixth Form): Years 12–13 (16–18 years old). The exams at the end are typically A levels, AS levels, NVQs or HNDs.

League-Tables

League-Tables are sometimes known as school performance tables and are based on children's attainment in School Attainment Tests (SATs), GCSEs and A levels. The better their results, the higher up the league table the school is placed. There is a great deal of debate about the value of league tables. The purpose of league tables was to offer information to parents that would allow them to make choices about which schools their children should attend. However, the degree to which parents can exercise this choice varies. Whereas the current system does allow parents to show their preferences for which schools their children should attend, their choices are often extremely limited because very often the best schools are full. In short, catchment areas often override choice and parents are forced to send their children to schools which they know to be poor performers. In recent years, and in reaction to severe criticism, the DCSF has introduced a value-added component to the formula to show how a school has improved the performance of its children. It is interesting to note that although Scotland, Wales and Northern Ireland still publish the results of individual schools, they have abolished league-tables.

Learning styles

The move towards catering for the individualized learning styles of children originated in the 1970s and has gained popularity in recent years. The assumption behind this initiative is that a person's preferred or dominant learning style is the method by which they are able to learn best. We all collect and process information through our five senses, but in very different ways, and it has been proposed that teachers should assess the learning styles of their children and adapt their classroom methods the better to fit each child's learning style. Thus the child is more likely to become engaged in the learning process and be fully motivated to achieve. As it is totally impractical to explore the vast range of learning-style models available to educationalists in a book such as this, we have chosen simply to describe the model that you are most likely to come across in your training – the sensory-preference model.

This model describes the three ways we use to absorb information and express ourselves. Our preferences may be visual, auditory or kinaesthetic in nature. **Auditory learning** occurs through hearing the spoken word. You need to make sure that you provide opportunities for your children to listen and respond to stimuli such as sound-effect CDs, radio broadcasts, talking books, song lyrics; and so on. **Kinaesthetic learning** occurs through doing and interacting, so you need to plan opportunities in your lessons for children to do such things as role play, card sorting, attitudinal exercises and sequencing activities. **Visual learning** occurs through looking at images, mind-maps, demonstrations and body language. You need to provide opportunities for children to produce their work in a visual manner, through such things as impact posters, newspaper frontispieces, creative drawing, and so on. In order to find out about the preferred learning styles of the children in your classes, it will be necessary for you to issue them with a questionnaire. There are numerous VAK (visual, auditory, kinaesthetic) questionnaires to be found online, but you need to be quite discriminating in order to select the right one for your children. You could try the following web addresses:

www.businessballs.com/vaklearningstylestest.htm

www.vark-learn.com/english/page.asp?p=questionnaire

Finally, below is a list of additional guidance on learning styles which will further inform your practice.

- If you notice that there are children who are not fully engaged in the learning process, ask them what you need to do to stimulate and motivate them.
- Although it is very important to cater for the preferred learning styles of the children in your classes, it is also very important to **challenge** them. Be overt in explaining the three sensory terms and outline the purpose of the activity. Inform the class as to whether the activity has been designed to **cater for** or **challenge** their learning styles.
- You need to be aware that most teachers teach their lessons in sympathy with their own preferred learning styles. This can have severe limitations on the breadth and balance of opportunities presented to their children. Our advice to you is to have a go at one of the VAK quizzes yourself, and challenge yourself to deliver your lessons in an unfamiliar style.

Multiple intelligences

The concept of multiple intelligences was introduced in 1983 by Howard Gardner who developed the theory that there was not just one intelligence but possibly seven. A description of these intelligences has been taken from the following web address www.infed.org/thinkers/gardner.htm and is outlined below.

Linguistic intelligence involves sensitivity to spoken and written language, the ability to learn languages and the capacity to use language to accomplish certain goals. This intelligence includes the ability to use language effectively to express oneself rhetorically or poetically; and language as a means to remember information. Writers, poets, lawyers and speakers are among those that Gardner sees as having high linguistic intelligence.

Logical-mathematical intelligence consists of the capacity to analyse problems logically, carry out mathematical operations and investigate issues scientifically. In Gardner's words, it entails the ability to detect patterns, reason deductively and think logically. This intelligence is most often associated with scientific and mathematical thinking.

Musical intelligence involves skill in the performance, composition and appreciation of musical patterns. It encompasses the capacity to recognize and compose musical pitches, tones and rhythms. According to Gardner, musical intelligence runs in an almost structural parallel to linguistic intelligence.

Bodily-kinaesthetic intelligence entails the potential of using one's whole body or parts of the body to solve problems. It is the ability to use mental abilities to coordinate bodily movements. Gardner sees mental and physical activity as related.

Spatial intelligence involves the potential to recognize and use the patterns of wide spaces, and more confined areas.

Interpersonal intelligence is concerned with the capacity to understand the intentions, motivations and desires of other people. It allows people to work effectively with others. Educators, salespeople, religious and political leaders and counsellors all need a well-developed interpersonal intelligence.

Intrapersonal intelligence entails the capacity to understand oneself, to appreciate one's feelings, fears and motivations. In Gardner's view it involves having an effective working model of ourselves, and to be able to use such information to regulate our lives.

The implications of the theory of multiple intelligences for your teaching are vast, but too many to take on board in a book such as this. Below are some suggestions as to how to improve your practice.

- Find out about the dominant intelligences of your children by asking them to fill in a simple questionnaire. There are numerous examples of these to be found on the internet. You might like to have a look at the web address shown below for an example of one of these; but you need to trawl through a number of sites in order to select the most appropriate questionnaire for your children: www.bgfl.org/bgfl/custom/resources_ftp/client_ftp/ks3/ict/multiple_int/questions/questions.cfm?lang=en.
- Have a go at completing the same questionnaire yourself. As is the case with learning styles, teachers tend to teach according to their dominant intelligence, and it is important that you challenge yourself as well as challenging the children.
- Use the information gathered from these questionnaires to plan activities which both cater for, and challenge, the dominant intelligences of your children.
- Make a point of giving status and credibility to the dominant intelligences of your children, especially the less able among them. Instead of asking yourself **whether** the child is intelligent, you need to ask yourself **how** they are intelligent. By doing this you will see the 'jokers', the 'carers' and the ones with 'ants in their pants' in a very different way.

National Curriculum

The National Curriculum was introduced into the educational system in 1988 as part of the Education Reform Act. The general directive of this initiative is that there should be uniformity in what is being learned by children in schools at the different stages of their development. You need to note that independent schools are not required to follow the National Curriculum. There are two principal aims to the National Curriculum:

- The school curriculum should aim to provide opportunities for all children to learn and achieve.
- The school curriculum should aim to promote children's spiritual, moral, social and cultural development and prepare all children for the opportunities, responsibilities and experiences of life.

The exam-based assessments, **National Curriculum** tests, are referred to as **SATs** (Standard Attainment Tests) and in primary schools these are given to the children in Years 2 and 6. You can find out more about the **National Curriculum** by logging on to the following website: http://curriculum.qca.org.uk/

Newly qualified teacher (NQT)

Newly qualified teachers are entitled to a teaching load that is 10 per cent lighter than other teachers in their schools. A reduced timetable has been ensured in order to allow for:

- regular meetings with their induction tutor
- progress reviews on a half-termly basis
- progress reviews with both the induction tutor and head teacher on a termly basis.

When you become an NQT, you need to make sure that you have been set targets that will help you to meet your induction standards and that you have been given a clear indication of your progress.

Office for Standards in Education (Ofsted)

Ofsted is a non-ministerial government department set up from the schools' inspectorate in 1992, to help improve the quality and standards of education. The mechanism through which this monitoring process occurs, is in Ofsted's independent inspections of schools and its advice to the Secretary of State for Education. Although its original function was to manage the system for inspecting state-run schools in England, its role has expanded. It is now responsible for reviewing the standards of local authorities, sixth-form and further education colleges, initial teacher-training courses, early years of childcare and education, and some independent schools and youth services.

The job of the Ofsted inspectors is to gather the information required to assess the educational performance of the school. This process involves collecting and analysing data, observing lessons, interviewing teachers and children, analysing children's work and meeting with parents and governors. The findings are published in a written report which must by law be made accessible to the parents of the children in the school. If a school is felt to be underperforming, it will be declared as having 'serious weaknesses' and any lack of improvement might put the school into 'special measures'. If improvements do not follow this course of action, then the school may be closed down under the 'Fresh Start' programme.

As a trainee teacher, your performances will not be subject to inspection by an Ofsted inspector. However, you need to be aware that it is a very stressful time for teachers and that this might affect the level of support you receive during the period of the inspection. You also need to be aware that some children pick up on the anxiety felt by teachers and other staff, and you need to reassure them that it is not they who are being assessed.

Planning, preparation and assessment (PPA) time

All teachers and trainees are entitled to time within the school week to carry out these administrative tasks.

Primary Framework

The Primary Framework has been designed to support teachers and schools to deliver high-quality learning and teaching for all children. It contains detailed guidance and materials to support literacy and mathematics in primary schools and other settings. More infomation can be found at the Standards site: www.standards.dscf.gov.uk/ primaryframeworks/

Professional development days

These training days are organized on a whole-school basis and are usually timed to occur at the beginning or the end of term, when disruption of school life can be kept to a minimum. Some schools disaggregate one or more of these days and carry out their professional development in twilight sessions after school. There are usually five of these days per year. As trainees you are highly likely to be required to attend, especially the ones at the start of your practice, since they will provide you with an opportunity to meet the staff and become acclimatized to the school.

Pupil referral unit (PRU)

PRUs have been designed for pupils who, for a variety of reasons (perhaps behavioural or emotional issues) have been excluded and who cannot for the time being attend a mainstream school. PRUs work closely with schools, parents, social services and other agencies in an attempt to help the child re-enter mainstream education.

Qualification and Curriculum Authority (QCA)

The QCA was established in 1997 and is responsible for standards in education, training and qualifications in schools, colleges and work.

Scaffolding

In the same way that scaffolding is constructed around a building in order to allow a builder to complete his or her tasks, learning is scaffolded when the teacher provides an infrastructure of support that allows children to complete the activities set before them. As a trainee, you may need to help your children get themselves organized, support and encourage them when they experience difficulties with their work, suggest the resources they might use, help to refocus them when they stray off task and/or provide keywords and/or pictures as hints to support their learning. However, what you must not do is actually complete the task for the child yourself.

Special educational needs coordinator (SENCO)

A SENCO is the member of staff who has responsibility for coordinating SEN provision within the school.

Standard Assessment Tests (SATs)

These tests are a form of summative assessment designed to measure a child's levels of knowledge, skills and understanding at the end of Key Stages 1, 2 and 3 in England and Key Stages 2 and 3 in Wales and Northern Ireland. Scotland tests children at similar ages, but these tests are conducted internally, and at a time when teachers feel that the children are ready for this assessment.

Teaching assistant (TA)

Teaching assistants are also known as learning assistants (LAs) and learning-support assistants (LSAs), and work under the direction of the class teacher. Many teaching assistants use their classroom experiences to support their applications to train as teachers. Teaching assistants may have general roles, or they may be allocated the responsibility of helping specific children with learning difficulties. Some TAs are given organizational responsibilities such as preparing resources and getting the classroom ready for learning. You will have the opportunity to work with one or more TAs in your school placements, and you need to build an effective working relationship with them. Make sure that you share your expectations of the class with them and clarify what you want them to do in each part of the lesson. You can do this by sharing your lesson plans with them and generally engaging them in dialogue about the children's learning and development.

Part Five
UNDERSTANDING YOUR TRAINING PROGRAMME

Understanding your training

11

So, you've done it – you've got on your course – congratulations. Now the hard work begins. The purpose of this chapter is twofold: to provide you with a broad overview of the nature and requirements of your training programme and to provide you with an opportunity to familiarize yourself with the QTS standards. It will be a very exciting year, but be prepared for lots of hard work and some real challenges.

Teaching is an all-consuming career. You must be willing and prepared to immerse yourself fully in your training for the duration of the course. If you have a non-teaching partner or children, then warn them of the workload you will have and the fact that this will impinge on your time together during the year ahead.

Having said how demanding your training is likely to be, you must be very careful that you do not become a workaholic. You do need to have an escape activity that will help you to reduce the stress and pressure of the job. You will have to plan time to see friends and family and to relax. Sometimes it is hard for your family to understand your workload, and we have both known trainees who have found this very difficult. You do have to remember that your course is a relatively short time compared with the exciting career you have ahead of you.

Whichever course you have chosen, you will spend time exploring the theories of learning and teaching, and you will then have to practise what you have learned. Teaching is a bit like juggling – there are lots of balls to keep in the air at once! It is obviously vital to get your planning right, but then there are all the other aspects to deal with at the same time in the classroom – behaviour-management, resources, time, deployment of teaching assistants, ICT, assessment, special needs, and so on. Just when you have got several of these in place, the one you thought you had got right now fails you! You have to develop patience, perseverance and belief in yourself.

Understanding and working towards the professional standards for QTS

12

Not only is it reasonable to expect your training provider to show an understanding of your needs as a trainee but it should also be expected to comply with the legal requirements associated with the assessment process. The following section has been written to clarify exactly what you need to do in order to gain qualified teacher status (QTS).

In order to gain QTS you are required to demonstrate full competence in all of the 33 Qualified Teacher Standards as prescribed by the Training and Development Agency (TDA). These standards have been laid out in Appendix 1. In your quest to realize these standards, you are required by the TDA and/or your training provider to spend a specific number of days in school during the course of your training. In addition, you must have at least two school placements. The number of days that you are required to spend in school depends upon the specific course you are undertaking. Details of these requirements can be seen below:

- A four-year undergraduate QTS programme   160 days (32 weeks)
- A two-or three-year QTS undergraduate programme   120 days (24 weeks)
- Graduate trainees on a primary PGCE programme   90 days (18 weeks)
- SCITT   90+ (determined by provider)
- An employment-based scheme   Determined by provider

In addition you must undertake placements in at least two schools and your provider must prepare you to teach across two or more consecutive age-ranges selected from the following:

- ages 3–5 (foundation stage)
- ages 5–7 (school years 1–2)
- ages 7–9 (school years 3–4)
- ages 9–11 (school years 5–6).

The provider must also give you the opportunity to engage with the expectations, curricula, strategies and teaching arrangements in the age-ranges immediately before and after the ones you are trained to teach. For example, if you are being trained to teach 5–9 year olds, you will have to undertake placements in Years 1 or 2, and then Years 3 or 4, as well as spending some time in the foundation stage and in a secondary school.

Although this is not the place to go into too much detail on this issue, you do need to know that the QTS standards form part of the framework of professional standards for teachers and some of the wider school workforce. You will encounter a set of induction standards when you become a newly qualified teacher (NQT), and there are also standards for Advanced Skills Teachers (ASTs) and headteachers.

Evidence to show that you have realized competence in the QTS standards is demonstrated in your teaching, through your portfolio, training-practice file, any reflective writing and school-practice reports. The QTS standards have been designed by experienced professionals, many of them teachers, in order to make sure that a range of potential experiences is made available to trainees throughout their training. Qualifying as a teacher is a privilege which should be earned and it is up to the trainees to prove beyond question their competence in the various standards.

It is absolutely vital that you gain an intimate understanding of the standards at the onset of your training period. Indeed, some courses expect you to complete pre-course assignments in relation to the standards. Professional standards at QTS level and at every subsequent level are divided into three main categories.

- professional attributes
- professional knowledge and understanding
- professional skills.

These standards provide clarity of the required expectations at each career stage. Before the QTS standards are explored in more detail, it is important to make the terms used transparent.

- The term **'learners'** is used instead of 'children and young people' when learning, per se, is the main focus of the standard. It refers to all children and young people, including those with particular needs, for example those with special educational needs, children in care, those for whom English is an additional language, those who are not reaching their potential, or those who are gifted and talented.
- The term **'colleagues'** is used for all those professionals with whom a teacher might work. It encompasses teaching colleagues, the wider workforce within an educational establishment, and also those from outside with whom teachers may be expected to have professional working relationships, for example early years and health professionals, and colleagues working in children's services.

- The term '**classroom**' is used to encompass all the settings within and beyond the workplace where teaching and learning take place.
- The term '**workplace**' refers to the range of educational establishments, contexts and settings (both inside and outside the classroom) where teaching takes place.
- The term '**subjects/curriculum areas**' is used to cover all forms of organized learning experienced across the curriculum, including the areas of learning in the foundation stage, play-based learning, cross-curricular themes and fully integrated thematic approaches.
- The terms '**lessons**' or '**sequences of lessons**' are used to cover teaching and learning activities wherever they take place, whatever their nature and length, and however they might be organized, and are applicable to all educational phases and contexts.
- The term '**well-being**' refers to the rights of children and young people (as set out and consulted upon in the *Every Child Matters*, and subsequently set out in the Children Act 2004, in relation to:

  – physical and mental health and emotional well-being
  – protection from harm and neglect
  – education, training and recreation
  – the contribution made by them to society
  – social and economic well-being.

- The term '**personalized learning**' means maintaining a focus on individual progress, in order to maximize all learners' capacity to learn, achieve and participate. This means supporting and challenging each learner to achieve national standards and gain the skills they need to thrive and succeed through-out their lives. Personalizing learning is **not** about individualization, where learners are taught separately or largely through a one-to-one approach.

Rather than presenting a list of QTS standards and then leaving you wondering exactly what you should do with these, we have provided detailed guidance to help you understand what each of the standards mean and to find the supporting evidence for your portfolio. You need to be aware that different training providers make variable use of the portfolio as an assessment tool. Your own provider may have its own idiosyncrasies as far as the role of the portfolio is concerned. You should also note that not all the QTS standards are observable, and you need to start collecting to find this non-classroom-based evidence as soon as possible. Figure 12.2 is a set of generalized guidance that will allow you to start collecting evidence early on in your training course. You do need to be aware that this menu of evidence is not exhaustive and there are bound to be numerous occasions when you will be able to come up with your own ideas on how to support your portfolio.

The way you present this portfolio evidence to your training provider is very important. It is not sufficient simply to place your documentation into your file without providing a context, rationale and reflective comment to accompany your evidence. Whoever is responsible for checking and/or moderating the portfolio will need to see the background information that supports the evidence, how and why it meets a particular standard, what you have learned from gathering this evidence and, most important of all, **how this new-found knowledge has impacted upon your professional practice.**

Although all ITT providers vary in their expectations of how the portfolio should be presented, the general principles described above will certainly be acceptable to all. Many training providers ask that a completed frontispiece be used to support each of the standards. An annotated example of one of these is shown in Figure 12.1. If the training provider has not been prescriptive in the way you present your portfolio standards you might like to consider this as a model.

This page should be placed in the portfolio as explanation of the evidence collected.

QTS standard achieved	Q11: Know the assessment requirements for the subjects/ curriculum areas in the age-ranges they are trained to teach, including those relating to public examinations and qualifications.
Evidence to support the standard	
Example of completed foundation-stage profile, with some teacher's notes which help form the evidence for the judgements.	
Written commentary on how KS1 SATs are carried out in my placement school, and some examples of moderated levelled writing completed with other schools in the pyramid.	
Copies of revision tasks completed by Year 6 children with targets showing how individuals can improve their work. My mentor and I have annotated these with the levels achieved so the children can understand them.	
Explanation of how the evidence supports the standard	
This first piece of evidence supports the standard by showing that I am aware of what reception teachers have to do in order to complete the foundation-stage profile and report this to parents.	
My notes show that I have a secure knowledge and understanding of the Key Stage 1 assessment requirements and arrangements.	
This shows I clearly know what is expected in KS2 SATs. By translating the National Curriculum assessment levels into 'child-speak', I have displayed a secure knowledge and understanding of the assessment criteria.	

You may wish to add to this initial reflection at a later date, in order to demonstrate progress throughout the course. If so, please complete a second copy of this sheet and get it signed by your professional tutor or your mentor.

Critically evaluate how this standard has impacted on your teaching/ professional development
Having to read through and become aquainted with the KS2 assessment in the core subjects has allowed me to become more proficient in assessing the performance of my children. This has resulted in me adopting a more confident approach towards my lessons. I feel that I am able to convey to the children that I know what is expected of them.
I also found it very useful to observe teachers undertaking KS1 SATs, and I learned how to carry out this process in a non-threatening way. It also helped me know where to pitch my teaching in KS1. Working with the reception teacher illustrated informal ways of assessing the children in all the areas of learning. I have used this approach while teaching older children.
Becoming familiar with the assessment criteria and arrangements has helped me to match up each child's performance with the appropriate level. Having done this, I have then used the results to inform my planning and set individual targets for all the children. Examples of how this has informed my lesson-planning can be seen in section Q26, while my target-setting can be seen in section Q28.
The true test of my understanding of the assessment came when I decided to abandon the formal language of the National Curriculum and translate the levels into language that is accessible to children. The response to this has been extremely positive. I have overheard children talking about what they have achieved and what they need to do next. This signifies to me that my efforts have paid off.

Date of reflection	
Signed	
Professional tutor/subject tutor (delete as applicable)	

Figure 12.1 Annotated example of reflection on the standard

By the end of the course trainees must provide evidence to demonstrate that they have met all the standards.

1. Suggested Sources of Portfolio Evidence

Those recommended for the award of QTS should:

	QTS standards	Suggested source of portfolio evidence	Support notes where appropriate
Q1	Have high expectations of children and young people including a commitment to ensuring that they can achieve their full educational potential and to establishing fair, respectful, trusting, supportive and constructive relationships with them.	Lesson-planning demonstrating use of prior attainment and special educational needs (SEN) data to set challenging learning and teaching objectives. Lesson-planning demonstrating how individuals' or groups' needs have been catered for. Lesson-planning with evidence of differentiated learning objectives being communicated to children. Lesson-observation feedback and evaluations. Evidence in marking and feedback to children. Lesson evaluations in which reflection on specific children/ issues takes place. Use of information in children's reports and progress checks to set their targets. Records of conversations with parents/carers/children and reflective comments.	This standard requires you to provide evidence to show that you hold high expectations of your children as far as their behaviour, attitudes and learning are concerned. Competence in this standard also means that you have demonstrated your understanding of the need to establish and maintain good working relationships with your children.

| Q2 | Demonstrate the positive values, attitudes and behaviour they expect from children and young people. | Lesson planning and observation feedback which highlights learning, behaviour and relationship issues.

Evaluations showing how conflicts are resolved.

Observation feedback showing respect for all children, good relationships with classes and consistency in the way they deal with learning and discipline issues.

Observation feedback showing creation of a 'can do' culture through questioning, praise, posters and so on.

Use of school and personal rewards/sanctions systems.

Photographs of classroom displays.

Evidence of punctuality, time management, personal organization and reliability.

Testimonials, letters or cards from parents or children | This standard requires you to show how you have acted as a role-model for your children. This standard could be realized in situations where you have demonstrated sensitive and effective ways to deal with conflict, or where you have helped to solve bullying or other personal issues. You may want to cite situations where you have used personal anecdotes or stories to highlight specific moral issues. You will easily be able to demonstrate this standard if you adopt an organized, caring and professional approach in your role as a teacher. |

| Q3 (a) | Be aware of the professional duties of teachers and the statutory framework within which they work. | Reflective and personalized notes on child protection, safeguarding children, anti-bullying and issues of 'disclosure'.

Reflective and personalized notes on restraint and/or medication issues.

Out-of-school trip organization procedure. Risk assessment.

Awareness of role of governing body.

Reflective and personalized annotations on the *Bristol Guide* (Lewis, 1998) a useful publication on statutory frameworks, obtainable from Bristol University.

Interview headteacher or chair of governors about these issues.

If you have been a governor yourself, you may have information from courses or briefing sessions. | You will note that this standard simply requires you to 'be aware' of these professional issues. Although the standard does not require you to provide evidence of how you have used this knowledge actually to carry out the duties. You are advised, wherever possible, to identify the potential implications for your professional practice. If you are able to personalize your annotation with examples from your own practice and/or experience, then so much the better. |

Communicating and working with others

| Q3 (b) | Be aware of the policies and practices of the workplace and share in collective responsibility for their implementation. | Contributions to events, extra-curricular activities, trips.

Annotation and implementation of school policies (for example health and safety, equal opportunities, SEN, child protection/safeguarding, anti-bullying) and reflective notes.

Personal, social and health education (PSHE) work on stereotyping, bullying and harassment.

Lesson-planning, observation feedback and evaluation.

Testimonial from appropriate staff. | Again, you need to show awareness of the content of the various planning and policy documents as well as providing evidence to show how you have worked with colleagues to implement some of these initiatives. |

Q4	Communicate effectively with children, young people, colleagues, parents and carers.	Lesson-observation feedback highlighting effective use of language to secure learning. Notes home to parents via logbooks, letters home and logs of telephone conversations. Notes from observing/contributing to parents' evening, review meeting or consultation meeting. Contributions to report-writing and progress checks. Evidence of working with TAs, HLTAs, technicians, librarians, teaching staff, contact with social workers, educational welfare officers, school nurse, educational psychologist and other children's services professionals. Work with visiting speakers.	You are advised to find at least one piece of evidence for each of these target groups to show how you communicate effectively with them.
Q5	Recognize and respect the contribution that colleagues, parents and carers can make to the development and well-being of children and young people and to raising their levels of attainment.	Knowledge of statutory rights of parents and carers (Bristol Guide). Notes home to parents via logbooks, letters home, logs of telephone conversations. Notes from observing/contributing to parents' evening, review meeting or consultation meeting. Understanding of the roles and evidence of working with TAs, HLTAs, technicians, librarians, teaching staff, social workers, educational welfare officers, school nurse, educational psychologist and other children's services professionals.	This standard is very similar to Q4, although in this case you simply have to find evidence to show that you recognize and respect the contribution of these three groups to the educational process. This is a 'find out all you can' exercise. Having said this, if you can personalize your annotations to illustrate how this new-found knowledge has impacted upon your practice and on the learning of children, then so much the better.

Q6	Have a commitment to collaboration and cooperative working.	Testimonial from mentor, head of department, TA or similar to show good working relationships with colleagues.	There is no reason why you cannot create your own proforma with a description of the Q6 standard on and list all the things you do to support and work with colleagues. Get each of them to add a comment and sign it.
		Preparation of resources/units of work with colleagues.	
		Team-teaching.	
		Contributions to concerts, presentations, extra-curricular activities.	
		Minutes of meeting (e.g. year group, key stage, whole staff) describing your specific contributions and how you have collaborated with colleagues.	

Personal professional development

| Q7 (a) | Reflect on and improve their practice, and take responsibility for identifying and meeting their developing professional needs. | The evidence needs to be in three parts for this standard:
Part One:
Lesson evaluations, reflections from discussions with colleagues, reflective journal entries.
Part Two:
The evidence that you have used this to improve your practice in lesson plans, observations, mentor/tutor meeting minutes, further evaluation.
Part Three:
Notes and reflections from involvement in school Continued Professional Development (CPD) activities.
Research carried out for assignments and/or completed assignments.
Subject-knowledge audit and action plans.
Examples of research or resources from, for instance subject associations, Qualification and Curriculum Authority, (QCA) *Times Educational Supplement* (*TES*) and so on, to help improve teaching and learning.
Arrange to work with other members of staff; attend a training course; visit another school according to your needs. | This is perhaps the most important of all the standards because the ability to reflect critically and act upon these reflections lies at the very heart of good teaching. You are required to demonstrate your ability to make judgements about the effectiveness of your teaching and then to improve it in some way. So your evidence will be both the reflection and the proof that you have improved. |

Q7 (b)	Identify priorities for their early professional development in the context of induction.	Subject-knowledge audit and action plans. Reflective comments on final trainee practice report. Career Entry and Development Profile completed at Transition Point 1 towards the end of final placement. Evidence of having arranged additional visits; e.g. special schools, and so on. Preparation for subject leadership in second year of teaching – course, reading, research.	This standard can only be completed towards the end of your training in preparation for the induction year as an NQT.
Q8	Have a creative and constructively critical approach towards innovation, being prepared to adapt their practice where benefits and improvements are identified.	Reflective journal entries. Lesson evaluations, observation feedback sheets, tutor-meeting logs. Notes and reflections from discussions with colleagues. Examples of research from, for example, subject associations, QCA, *TES* and so on, to help improve teaching and learning. Research for assignments and completed assignments. Notes and reflections from involvement in school CPD activities. For example, sessions on the creative teaching of fractions, which you have then used in your classroom. Comments on teaching practice; report about use of creative approaches.	You need to be able to demonstrate that you are open to new ideas and that you have used these to develop your practice.

| Q9 | Act upon advice and feedback and be open to coaching and mentoring. | Reflective journal entries.

Lesson evaluations, observation feedback sheets, tutor-meeting logs.

Notes and reflections from discussions with colleagues.

Trainee practice reports.

Testimonial from mentor. | The key thing to note here is that it is all well and good you listening to advice and guidance from your colleagues, but if you do not act upon this then the process has been in vain. You need to show how you have used this advice/guidance offered by your colleagues to support your practice.

You also need to demonstrate that you can be 'coached' as well as mentored, in other words solve problems yourself, and show willingness to suggest solutions and try alternatives. |

2. Professional knowledge and understanding

Those recommended for the award of QTS should:

	QTS	Source of portfolio evidence	Supporting notes where appropriate
Teaching and Learning			
Q10	Have a knowledge and understanding of a range of teaching, learning and behaviour-management strategies and know how to use and adapt them, including how to personalize learning and provide opportunities for all learners to achieve their potential.	Lesson-planning, evaluation and observation feedback. Effective questioning technique as demonstrated in lesson observations. Effective use of praise. Selection and delivery of appropriate curriculum content and differentiated tasks. Assignments. Use of behaviour policy and behaviour plans for individual children. Evidence of implementation of behaviour-management training session materials. Personalized annotations to training on behaviour-management handouts. Arrangements for seating within the class or on the carpet, and for lining up. Effective use of different organizational strategies in lessons to support learning. Exploration of children's learning styles/intelligences and implementation of this information in lesson planning.	This standard is pretty straightforward but we would advise you to provide evidence that covers each of the three elements: teaching, learning and behaviour management. You need to ensure that you demonstrate a knowledge and understanding of the ways in which you can personalize learning.

Assessment and monitoring

Q11	Know the assessment requirements and arrangements for the subjects/curriculum areas in the age-ranges they are trained to teach, including those relating to public examinations and qualifications.	Notes on or annotated sections of the National Curriculum. Assessment criteria produced in 'child-speak'. Contributions to moderation of work. Evidence of use of level descriptors. Marking of SATs or practice papers; analysis of optional SATs. Notes on foundation-stage profile and how this is completed.	For this standard you are required to demonstrate a secure understanding of the assessment frameworks in which your children are working. You can demonstrate this in a number of ways: by presenting and annotating any research you have conducted, or by demonstrating your proficiency in working to these assessment criteria.
Q12	Know a range of approaches to assessment, including the importance of formative assessment.	Lesson-planning, evaluation and feedback. Evidence of use of assessment for learning (AfL) techniques. Formative marking of children's work. Evidence of oral assessment and feedback. Marked tests and feedback. Peer-assessment opportunities in lesson plan/observation. Target-setting.	Again, this standard is quite straightforward, but you are strongly advised to present a range of assessment techniques in your portfolio. You also need to demonstrate an ability to monitor the progress of children and use your judgement to intervene in order to enable them to succeed.
Q13	Know how to use local and national statistical information to evaluate the effectiveness of their teaching, to monitor the progress of those they teach and to raise levels of attainment.	Lesson-planning, evaluation and observation feedback. Use of prior attainment data in lesson planning (SATs results, reading and maths scores, children's learning styles). Use of targets for children/groups. Records of assessment in mark-book. Notes on how to use statistical data from mentor meetings.	In order to realize this particular standard you need to do three things: first, research and present your data; second, show how you have used this to plan for differentiation in your lessons; third, show how you have used this data to evaluate your children's achievement and progress.

Subjects and curriculum

Q14	Have a secure knowledge and understanding of their subjects/ curriculum areas and related pedagogy to enable them to teach effectively across the age and ability range for which they are trained.	Subject knowledge audit and action plans. Lesson-planning, observation feedback, evaluations. Evidence from question-and-answer sessions, extension tasks. Marking of children's work and feedback. Appropriate use of ICT. Annotated handouts from training courses. Evidence of awareness and use of the national strategy approaches in teaching. Assignments. Testimonials from key staff.	You need to know that subject knowledge is an absolute priority of the TDA and you should do everything you can to show progression in this aspect of your training and how you have identified specific areas for development. You then need to take this a stage further by demonstrating how these specific weaknesses have been successfully addressed. We need to stress that this standard is not just about how much subject knowledge you have personally but how well you can impart this to your children. (i.e. pedagogy) You need to demonstrate this across all curriculum subjects.

Literacy, numeracy and ICT

Q15	Know and understand the relevant statutory and non-statutory curricula, frameworks, including those provided through the national strategies, for their subjects/ curriculum areas, and other relevant initiatives applicable to the age and ability range for which they are trained.	Lesson-planning, observation feedback, evaluations. Evidence in planning using literacy and numeracy frameworks. Evidence of planning and teaching programmes such as SEAL. Evidence in planning to show how EYFS guidance is used. Assignments. Annotated programmes in connections with initiatives in PSHE, citizenship, community cohesion, thinking skills, and so on.	When planning your lessons you are strongly advised to provide links with such initiatives as the literacy and numeracy frameworks.

Q16	Have passed the professional skills tests in numeracy, literacy and information and communication technology (ICT).	Copies of certificates obtained from test centre when tests are passed.	You are strongly advised to book up early for these tests. You can practise these tests online by logging on to the TDA website. Alternatively you could read the following publications: Johnson (2003) Ferrigan (2004) Patmore (2004)
Q17	Know how to use skills in literacy, numeracy and ICT to support their teaching and wider professional activities.	Lesson-planning, evaluations, observation feedback. Records of children's progress – mark-sheets. Use of the internet, digital cameras, PowerPoint presentations, interactive whiteboard. Use of ICT for reports and progress checks. Preparation of appropriate resources using literacy and/or numeracy skills. Database work – use of spreadsheets.	The TDA is again looking for a range of evidence here. You need, therefore, to select evidence from each of the three elements described in the standard: literacy, numeracy and ICT.

Achievement and diversity

Q18	Understand how children and young people develop and that the progress and well-being of learners are affected by a range of developmental, social, religious, ethnic, cultural and linguistic influences.	Lesson-planning, observation feedback, evaluations, logs of tutor meetings. Selection of relevant topics for lesson content. Contact with mentor, SENCO, other agencies about children with social/emotional difficulties and evidence of children with social or emotional problems being catered for. Notes from discussion with SENCO about, e.g., autism, ADHD, dyslexia, Asperger's syndrome. Example of IEP and its implications. Awareness of issues facing children from a variety of backgrounds and cultures – English as an additional language (EAL) policy, working with EAL coordinators, differentiated objectives, worksheets, and so on. Research assignments. Annotated handouts from EAL training session. Case studies of individual children.	To realize Q18 you simply need to demonstrate that you have an understanding of how the learning of children is affected by the various elements described in the standard. This is also the place to link your 'learning theories' work to your work in the classroom. You can do this by identifying the potential implications of this knowledge on your practice and/or by describing your professional experiences.

Q19	Know how to make effective personalized provision for those they teach, including those for whom English is an additional language or who have special educational needs or disabilities, and how to take practical account of diversity and promote equality and inclusion in their teaching.	Lesson-planning, observation feedback, evaluations, logs of tutor meetings. Examples of differentiated tasks and resources, and evaluations of their use. Evaluation of use of supportive techniques – e.g. writing-frames, and so on. Notes from meetings with EAL coordinator and reflection/ implications. Multi-cultural displays. Examples of children's work. Completed tasks or notes from EAL training sessions. Use of TAs and support teachers in lessons. Use of prior attainment and SEN data. Assignments. Notes from discussion with SENCO about autism, ADHD, dyslexia, Asperger's syndrome, and so on. Testimonial from appropriate staff. Example of an individual education plan (IEP) and its implications.	Again, the TDA is looking for a range of evidence here. Take each element described in the standard and present at least one separate piece of evidence for each.
Q20	Know and understand the roles of colleagues with specific responsibilities, including those with responsibility for learners with special educational needs and disabilities and other individual learning needs.	Notes from discussion with SENCO, annotated SEN Code of Practice and SEN policy. Notes from discussion with other members of staff, e.g. assessment coordinator, subject leaders, G and T (gifted and talented) coordinator. Evidence of working with TAs, HLTAs, EAL coordinator. Assignments.	Whenever you go to a new school it is vital to find out what people in the school actually do. Select a few core staff and make it your business to interview them with a view to finding out how their roles impact upon your professional practice.

Health and well-being

Q21 (a)	Be aware of current legal requirements, national policies and guidance on the safeguarding and promotion of the well-being of children and young people.	Certificate from safeguarding/child-protection training.	This is a difficult standard to meet as there are so many national, county- and school-based policies relating to the safeguarding and promotion of well-being of children and young people. It is extremely important that you demonstrate an awareness of any developments in this field at a national, LA and/or school level. You will note that the standard stresses your need to 'be aware' of the current legal requirements, and so on. You can show this by annotating and, wherever possible, by linking the information provided to your own professional experiences or by outlining the potential implications of this new-found knowledge for your professional practice.
		School child-protection documentation – annotated with implications for own practice.	
		Accident reports, issues of 'disclosure' and reflections.	
		Restraint issues, medication issues.	
		Out-of-school trip organizations procedure.	
		Personalized annotations of sections of the Bristol Guide.	
		Personalized annotations of the Every Child Matters agenda	
		Personalized annotations of the Children's Act.	

| Q21 (b) | Know how to identify and support children and young people whose progress, development or well-being is affected by changes or difficulties in their personal circumstances, and when to refer them to colleagues for specialist support. | Evidence of discussion with mentor, SENCO and parents about children who have faced recent changes in their life: e.g., bereavement, divorce, move, bullying, new baby, and so on. Use of TAs and support teachers in lessons in response to individual circumstances. Evidence of working with TAs, HLTAs, contact with social workers, educational welfare officers, school nurse, educational psychologist and other children's services professionals. | In order to realize this particular standard, you need to show that you are aware of the procedural protocol required to support your children in the circumstances described. |

3. Professional skills

Those recommended for the award of QTS should:

	QTS standards	Source of portfolio evidence	Supporting notes where appropriate
Q22	Plan for progression across the age and ability range for which they are trained, designing effective learning sequences within lessons and across series of lessons and demonstrating secure subject/curriculum knowledge.	Lesson-planning. Schemes/units of work – medium-term plans you have written, modified or adapted. Assignments. Planning includes detailed and relevant differentiated learning objectives and evidence of differentiated tasks.	You should be able to provide evidence for this standard with your day-to-day planning and teaching. You should ensure you include sequences of lessons which show progression.
Q23	Design opportunities for learners to develop their literacy, numeracy and ICT skills.	Lesson planning Schemes/units of work – medium-term plans. Assignments. Examples of marked children's work and evaluation of effectiveness of activity. Internet research tasks.	Again, the TDA is looking for a range of evidence here. Provide at least one piece of evidence to cater for each of the elements described in the standard.

Q24	Plan homework or other out-of-class work to sustain learners' progress and to extend and consolidate their learning.	Lesson-planning or observation feedback which details homework set. Evidence of extension work for children, e.g. research tasks and evaluation. Fieldwork tasks and evaluation. Examples of marked homework tasks and evaluation of effectiveness of activity. Effective plans for activities in school grounds (e.g. gardening/environmental/weather), or on visits or within clubs.	This should not be evidenced merely by what has been planned. It would be worthwhile to include examples of completed work and your evaluation of how the activity sustained or extended the children's learning.
Q25	Teach lessons and sequences of lessons across the age and ability range for which they are trained in which they:		
Q25 (a)	Use a range of teaching strategies and resources, including e-learning, taking practical account of diversity and promoting equality and inclusion;	Lesson-planning, observation feedback, evaluations. Evidence of variety of teaching strategies in lessons. Effective and safe use of a range of resources. Effective use of ICT by children. Use of e-learning: e.g. activities on school website or virtual learning environment (VLE).	The keyword here is 'range', in relation to strategies and resources, while at the same time ensuring inclusion of all children.
Q25 (b)	Build on prior knowledge, develop concepts and processes, enable learners to apply new knowledge, understanding and skills and meet learning objectives;	Lesson-planning, observation feedback, evaluations. Use of prior attainment data in planning. Evidence of appropriate activities to allow children to apply what they have learned. Observation with particular focus on start of lesson and how assessment has been used in planning. The 'context' section of a newly created scheme of work.	This standard has links with Q13 and you could cross-reference some of the evidence from this standard.

Q25(c)	Adapt their language to suit the learners they teach, introducing new ideas and concepts clearly, and using explanations, questions, discussions and plenaries effectively.	Observation feedback and evaluations highlighting effective communication with children. Observation feedback and evaluations highlighting effective use of questioning. Observation feedback and evaluations highlighting effective use of plenary session.	This standard can really only be evidenced through lesson observation.
Q25(d)	Manage the learning of individuals, groups and whole classes, modifying their teaching to suit the stage of the lesson.	Effective use of group work, pair work and a variety of teaching strategies. Use of individual and group research tasks. Evidence of pace and purpose in lessons. Effective use of behavioural-management strategies.	With all these examples, you need to demonstrate that you modify your teaching to suit the stage of the lesson. For example, clear engagement at the beginning and management of groups while monitoring the whole class (e.g. scanning, no queues). You need to provide evidence that you can manage individual learning, whole-class learning and group learning.

Assessing, monitoring and giving feedback

Q26 (a)	Make effective use of a range of assessment, monitoring and recording strategies.	Observation feedback, evaluations. Formative marking of children's work. Evidence of oral assessment and feedback. Moderation of children's work. Marked tests and feedback. Peer-assessment tasks and evaluation. Target-setting. Evidence of effective use of questioning. Examples of self-assessment sheets. Use of plenary session. Mark-book/assessment grids. Contributions to report-writing and progress checks.	This standard is linked with Q11 and Q12, and if you have previously provided evidence to show how you have implemented your newly discovered knowledge of assessment strategies, you may be able to cross-reference these in order to meet this standard.
Q26 (b)	Assess the learning needs of those they teach in order to set challenging learning objectives.	Lesson-planning as a result of assessment. Evaluations that specifically link the assessment of children's learning with learning objectives for future lessons. Formative marking of children's work with reflections about implications for future lesson-planning. Target-setting. Self-assessment sheets and reflections about implications for future lesson-planning. Effective use of plenary session to assess learning and plan next lesson. Use of knowledge of children's learning styles to set differentiated and challenging work. Assignments.	The main purpose of this standard is to get you to use your own assessment data to inform your planning. In order to realize this standard you need to make the links between your assessment and planning absolutely transparent.

Q27	Provide timely, accurate and constructive feedback on learners' attainment, progress and areas for development.	Lesson-observation feedback detailing the feedback you have given. Formative marking of children's work. Contributions to progress checks.	The TDA is again looking for a range of evidence to support this standard.
Q28	Support and guide learners to reflect on their learning, identify the progress they have made and identify their emerging learning needs.	Lesson-observation feedback. Effective use of questioning. Self-assessment sheets completed by children. Use of plenary sessions. Examples of children using meta-cognitive processes. Assignments. Evidence of children using their own learning logs.	There is no reason why you cannot employ a reflective strategy similar to the one described to you later on in this chapter. The formula is appropriate and transferable to all levels of education.

Reviewing teaching and learning

Q29	Evaluate the impact of their teaching on the progress of all learners, and modify their planning and classroom practice where necessary.	Lesson evaluations, observation feedback, logs of tutor meetings. Reflective journal. Notes and reflections from discussions with colleagues. Questionnaires completed by children. Logs of tutor meeting showing responses to feedback. Assignments.	This standard is similar to Q7(a). You have to demonstrate that your teaching helped all children to learn. You must also show that not only have you evaluated, but that you have modified your planning as a result.

Learning environment			
Q30	Establish a purposeful and safe learning environment conducive to learning and identify opportunities for learners to learn in out-of-school contexts.	Observation feedback. Evidence of teaching assertively, with pace and purpose; good use of body language and voice tone; effective use of praise; selection of appropriate tasks. Evidence of good working relationships with children. Evidence of implementation of school behavioural policy. Evidence of use of effective grouping strategies. School trips – evidence of assisting with these and associated reflections. Evidence of having created a 'can do' culture through classroom displays.	Most of the evidence for this standard will come from lesson observations. You are also advised to log your contributions to the 'out-of-school context' scenarios and ask your colleagues to comment on and sign to verify this input.
Q31	Establish a clear framework for classroom discipline to manage learners' behaviour constructively and promote their self-control and independence.	Observation feedbacks. Evidence of implementation of school behavioural policy. Evidence of dealing with individual children.	This is a very important standard, and it is important that your mentor is ensuring you achieve this as soon as possible.
Team working and collaboration			
Q32	Work as a team member and identify opportunities for working with colleagues, sharing the development of effective practice with them.	Testimonial from support staff. Evidence of joint planning, team-teaching and contribution to team or whole-school meetings. Contribution to working parties. Working with colleagues in CPD sessions.	It is not enough to provide evidence that you have attended meetings. You need to demonstrate that you are actively working with others – making contributions, building on ideas, sharing things you have done, asking for advice, and so on.

Q33	Ensure that colleagues working with them are appropriately involved in supporting learning and understand the roles they are expected to fulfil.	Observation feedback. Written communications with TA, HLTA, technician, librarian or supply teachers. Evidence from lesson plans. Testimonial from support staff. Evidence of effective deployment of support staff. Assignments.	The notion behind insisting that you gain competence in this standard is to help you to be proactive in establishing and maintaining effective working relationships with colleagues. Include your colleagues in the planning and evaluation stages of your lessons.

Figure 12.2 Suggested evidence for portfolio

Becoming a reflective practitioner

13

The term 'reflective practice' introduced by Donald Schön in his book *The Reflective Practitioner* (1983), lies at the very heart of every intial teacher-training course. According to Schön, reflective practice is the process of thoughtfully considering one's own experiences in applying knowledge to practice while being coached by professionals in the discipline. In education, it refers to the process of the teacher studying his or her own teaching methods and determining what works best for the children. At a later stage in your career, you may be interested in exploring the numerous interpretations of the notion of reflective practice. The rationale for focusing on Schön's work is that his ideas have been extremely influential in initial teacher training in Britain in recent years. Indeed, two of the QTS standards are related to reflection:

> Q7(a) Reflect on and improve their practice, and take responsibility for identifying and meeting their developing professional needs.
>
> Q29 Evaluate the impact of their teaching on the progress of all learners, and modify their planning and classroom practice where necessary.

Schön (1983), cited in Furlong and Maynard (1995), emphasizes that teachers have to cope with the fact that no two groups of children are alike and that even with individuals with whom they are familiar, they are constantly having to present new material to them. This inevitably creates its own unique problems in terms of explanation and understanding. The teacher has constantly to reflect upon, and react to, the ever-changing scenarios that occur in his or her classroom in such a way that the process appears to be seamless to the class. Schön called this process 'reflection-*in*-action'. Reflection-*in*-action occurs when a practitioner faces an unknown situation. In these circumstances, the practitioner is able to bring certain aspects of her work to her level of consciousness, to reflect upon it and reshape it without interrupting the flow of proceedings. It is fair to say that many experienced teachers do this quite naturally and intuitively without giving the process a great deal of thought. However, this process does not come naturally to new teachers, be they trainee or NQT, and they tend to get somewhat flustered when new scenarios are presented to them and things do not quite go according to plan. If this happens to you, try not to worry too much – things will get better with experience. The key point is to learn from it. Some of the unpredictable and untoward things that are likely to throw you off course in the initial stages of your teaching will be of little or no consequence as you become more used to the role. Having said this, you still need to practise the skill of flexibility in your lessons.

Reflection-*in*-action largely involves 'situated knowledge' and is a process that we often go through without necessarily being able to say exactly what we are doing. Reflecting on, and articulating our thoughts about our teaching **after** the lesson has happened, is called 'reflection-*on*-action', and it is something that many teachers find challenging. They find it difficult to articulate all the things they do intuitively in the classroom to produce a good lesson. The authors are both in agreement with Schön who believed passionately that reflection-*on*-action is a key process in learning how to teach. Schön (1983), argues that no matter how inadequate trainees' verbal reconstruction of events may be, it is only by constantly bringing the ways in which they are framing their teaching situations to their level of consciousness, that they will eventually gain control of their own teaching. The following quote from Schön (1987) cited in Furlong and Maynard (1995), makes the point clearly:

> As I think back on my experience … I may consolidate my understanding of the problem or invent a better or more general solution to it. If I do, my present reflection on my earlier reflection-in-action begins a dialogue of thinking and doing through which I become more skilful.

All ITT providers will encourage reflection-*in*-action in order to help you to move towards these standards. They will also insist that some kind of reflection-*on*-action takes place in the form of a reflective journal or series of lesson evaluations. Using this 'reflection-*on*-action' process as a model, Gererd has worked with a colleague to create a reflective formula which is currently used by trainees in two ITT programmes. The general principles underlying the formula are shown in Figure 13.1.

The first column in the reflective formula requires you simply to **describe** the professional scenario presented to you. This could be something that happened in the classroom, an incident in the school corridor or your observations of interactions between colleagues and children. At this point in the reflective process, there is no evaluative input whatsoever – you simply need to describe the scenario. Having done this, you now need to describe the perceived consequences of what you have just experienced; in other words, what happened as a result of the scenario. For example, you may have noticed that in one of your observations of a science lesson that a teacher failed to establish his expectations, rules and sanctions before allowing the children to undertake a practical investigation. The consequences of not doing this might have been that the children behaved in an unruly fashion, thus disrupting learning in the lesson. Another consequence could have been that health and safety rules were breached and that an accident occurred. These crucial decision-making factors in a lesson can be called 'watershed moments' because they represent specific points in lessons where teachers' actions or inactions can lead to varying and sometimes diverse consequences (Dixie, 2007). You will also note from the formula that this is the place to describe your emotional responses to the scenarios presented to you. In Dixie (2005, 2007), Gererd gives a high profile to the importance of exploring the emotional side of teaching. Recognizing and dealing with your emotional responses to teaching is an important part of the reflective process.

Experience shows us that most trainees are quite adept at describing professional scenarios but far less skilled at recognizing watershed moments and/or the potential consequences of these. In most cases, this is where their reflective practice usually ends. Unless challenged, most trainees do not take the process any further. They neither identify the implications of their teaching experiences nor do they show how they have modified or altered their practice in the light of their reflections. If the reflective cycle illustrated in Figure 13.1 and Table 13.1 is to be successfully realized then the requirements outlined in columns 3 and 4 need to be fulfilled. Having responded to your reflections by taking the appropriate action, the whole reflective process starts over again. This document does not have to be completed electronically, nor does it have to be completed in the column form presented in the formula. It is, however, very important that the criteria in all four stages are met if you want to demonstrate your skill as a reflective practitioner and realize the standards which have been presented to you overleaf. Exemplars of three reflective logs are provided to support theoretical diagrams shown in Figure 13.1.

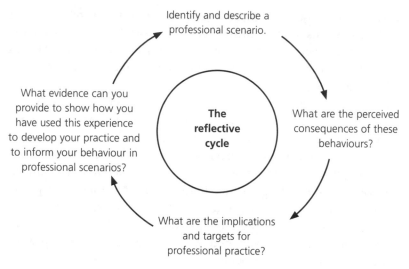

Identify and describe a
professional scenario.

What evidence can you
provide to show how you
have used this experience
to develop your practice and
to inform your behaviour in
professional scenarios?

**The
reflective
cycle**

What are the perceived
consequences of these
behaviours?

What are the implications
and targets for
professional practice?

Table 13.1 Reflective formula

Identification/description of professional scenarios
• Lesson observation
• Out-of-classroom scenarios
• Interaction with colleague(s)
• Interaction with parents/carers
What happened?

What are the perceived consequences of these behaviours?

• Identify teaching and learning consequences by looking for 'watershed' moments.
• Identify the emotional consequences for you as a teacher. Did the incident make you feel proud, angry, disappointed, disempowered, and so on?

What were the consequences?

Implications and targets for professional practice

• How will you use this information to inform your professional practice?
• What targets will you set yourself?
• What strategies will you use?
• How are you going to use the emotional consequences to inform your future practice?

What will you do?

Provide evidence showing how you have used this experience to develop your professional practice. Make overt reference to a professional standard.

You may complete this column at a later date.

Write about how you have changed your practice as a result of the reflection.

Trainee X: Extract from reflective journal

Identification/description of professional scenarios

In a recent numeracy lesson with Year 1 I had planned a whole range of activities around recognizing and writing numbers to 30.

The children had been very 'high' before break, with my mentor having to work really hard to keep them under control.

In this particular lesson I made the mistake of not prefacing the activity with my expectations and I did not use praise to settle them and show what was required. Instead, I plunged headlong into the lesson. I took too long to get the children into a circle for the first activity. Then I asked them to all turn to a different direction on the carpet to see the whiteboard, then again to face my number line.

I also made the mistake of allowing the children to call out answers, and then getting individuals to the front. I did not use sanctions.

Perceived consequences of these behaviours

I became obsessed with managing all the activities rather than controlling their behaviour.

The children spent most of the time moving round the carpet. They ended up spending 35 minutes on the carpet. This meant they were fidgety and could not concentrate. I was doing all the work.

Behaviour disintegrated and very little learning took place. Children felt they could do what they liked.

Implications and targets for professional practice

I must be alert to what is going on – read the children's reactions.

I should revisit rules and expectations when needed. Once on the carpet, it is not good use of time to move them around.

I must insist children put their hands up, and not take answers from those who call out. I must use sanctions, and then children will know they cannot get away with anything.

Provide evidence showing how you have used this experience to develop your professional practice. How do know whether you have been successful?

After lunch the class teacher and I both made our expectations plain. I gave a sanction to P by writing his name on the board. This seemed to shock the whole class and they immediately focused on me, even sitting up straighter and improving eye contact.

I kept my eye on the clock and made sure we only spent 15 minutes on the carpet. The children had plenty of time to complete their learning activities. I felt as though it was the children that had worked hard, not me.

Trainee Y: Extract from reflective journal

Identification/description of professional scenarios

This week I conducted several observations with the purpose of observing a range of teachers in a variety of year groups and subjects. The focus of these observations was effective behaviour management.

Perceived consequences of these behaviours

Having made my observations, I then identified common strategies for good behaviour management. I was quite surprised to see that so many children in these observed classes were clear about what was expected from them in terms of their behaviour. This was noticeable even when the children entered the classroom. Having discussed this issue with the teachers, I am certain that their good behaviour was a result of the rules and consequences being established and reinforced so early on. In situations where the school's behaviour policy was used, teachers were only successful in gaining discipline in their classes when this was supported by assertive body language, tone of voice and a consistent approach towards the offences. Children also behaved well in classes where teacher praise was abundant and where a 'can do' climate had been established.

Implications and targets for professional practice

When I begin teaching next week I will ensure that I start all my lessons by outlining my expectations to the children and by making my rules, rewards and consequences transparent.

I won't be afraid to use sanctions, but will focus first and foremost on the use of praise.

Provide evidence showing how you have used this experience to develop your professional practice

I have already taught four lessons. I have introduced my expectations to the children in an assertive and robust manner. I have my rules clearly displayed on laminated sheets at the front of the room. We have discussed the class rules and sanctions.

Although the behaviour of the children in my lessons has not been perfect, I am generally pleased with the way my lessons have gone. I still need to use praise more freely. I was reluctant to use sanctions, but did so today. It really helped me remain 'in charge'.

Trainee Z: Extract from reflective journal

Identification/description of professional scenarios

Today I taught a PSHE lesson. I used the SEAL plans and stuck to them quite rigidly as I am only in the second week of my placement with Year 5 children. I got them to reflect on various situations involving 'conflict' and asked them to come up with ways of heating up or cooling down the conflict. I then asked them to share their ideas, and eventually got them to design a poster detailing these. My plenary involved a scenario in which they had to apply the knowledge they had gained.

Perceived consequences of these behaviours

I felt the class responded well, but was not sure they learned very much. I was unsure about how much 'input' I should have had. I think they may just have consolidated and brought to the surface things they knew already. They did not really use any new vocabulary or discuss other conflicts such as those involving war or religious disagreement.

Implications and targets for professional practice

I must make sure my subject knowledge is several steps ahead of the children's. I must make sure I list key vocabulary and questions on my lesson plan. I could ask children before the lesson what they know already about these themes, so I know where they need to go. I must have high expectations of them and use extended vocabulary which they probably hear on the news anyway. I must not be afraid to 'teach from the front' and to give them new strategies.

Provide evidence showing how you have used this experience to develop your professional practice. How do you know whether you have been successful?

I taught the next lesson in the series and linked it to conflict in other parts of the world. I used rich vocabulary such as resolution, peace-keepers, negotiation and diplomacy. The children were much more engaged in the lesson and referred to things they had heard about outside school. They wanted to talk well into break-time, and two children brought in further information the next day. At a parents' evening soon afterwards, one parent commented on how their son had come home and talked about this lesson and how it had helped him with a friendship issue.

Figure 13.2 Three extracts from reflective journals

How to get the most out of attending lectures, presentations and workshops

14

Although all ITT programmes contain elements of theory in their training, the degree to which this occurs depends very much on the nature of the programme and on the specific requirements of the training provider. Although many of you will be simply itching to get to work in the classroom, do not underestimate the importance of knowing about, understanding and being able to apply educational theory to your practice. Most of this theoretical input will be formally offered to you in lectures, presentations and workshops, and it is vital that you recognize the importance of these opportunities in helping to support your pedagogic practice. The best trainees are those who successfully link the theory of teaching to their everyday practice. In addition to providing you with a theoretical perspective to your teaching, these sessions will also be an important conduit for disseminating practical and logistical information about the requirements of the course. They are also a vital arena for sharing ideas and discussing issues with fellow trainees. This is what most trainees enjoy most of all. A range of advice is provided below to help you to get the most out of these sessions.

- Always approach your training sessions with an open mind. Some of us become very entrenched in our views, so try to be receptive to new ideas and prepared to try these out in the classroom. If these are not immediately successful, do not simply dismiss them out of hand – it could be that you are not quite ready for these strategies to work yet.
- Lecturers and trainers hold their own value systems which may be at odds with your own. Make sure that you critically evaluate what is being presented to you and be prepared to justify your opinions of the issues being discussed.
- Believe it or not, lecturers/trainers depend heavily on you making a contribution to their sessions. Do not be afraid to ask questions, to challenge their assertions in an appropriate manner and/or to relate the content of the discussion to your own professional experiences.

- Remember that the information gathered is only useful if it is easily available to you when you want to access it. Make detailed notes and store them appropriately because you never know when you will need them. Using ring-binders with dividers to organize your work can save you a lot of time in the long-run.
- Use sessions to clarify your own understanding. While you have experienced professionals in the room, ask questions, seek advice, ask for suggestions and clarify anything you are not sure about. Be assured that someone else will also want to know the answer!

15 Essays and assignments

Completing assignments and tasks provides you with the opportunity to draw good links between theory and practice, and to tie together all the learning from lectures and placements. Having to draw your own conclusions will help you to formulate your own views and ideas with more confidence. Trainees often find that they use information from assignments later in their careers, so keep them in a safe place! Moreover, these assignments give your course leaders the opportunity to assess your knowledge and understanding and provide you with evidence for many of the standards.

You will probably have to produce a range of essays and assignments during your training, some of which will be prescribed and some of which you will be given a choice of topic. Some providers are very creative in the way they assess trainees. They may include presentations, action research, video capture or practical projects in their courses. If you are given a choice over subject matter, you could consider any of the following:

- behaviour management
- differentiation
- learning styles
- learning theories
- inclusion
- assessment for learning
- personalized learning.

Formal assignment writing is not usually too much of a problem for those trainees who have taken a traditional route through education via sixth form and university before starting their teacher-training course. However, for those trainees who have had an extended time away from the educational system, even thinking about writing an essay/assignment can be a traumatic event. With this in mind, we have provided a number of tips which we hope will support those of you to whom academic work does not come easily.

- In situations where you have a choice, select a topic that interests you.
- Carry out a portfolio check to see which standards you are struggling to meet, and target your assignment accordingly. If, for example, you have been placed in a school in a predominantly white, middle-class catchment area, then you may struggle to find evidence to meet Q18 and Q19 which relate to the issue of culture, ethnicity and social background. You might, therefore, like to consider producing an assignment on ethnic diversity and inclusion/achievement.
- Don't prevaricate! Start reading around the topic as soon as you can after receiving the assignment instructions. Leaving things until the last minute never works.
- Discuss your essay topic and title with your tutors and fellow trainees. Doing so can provide you with different perspectives, help you to get your own thoughts in order and provide greater focus.
- Make sure that you fully understand and meet the assessment criteria. Do not do what we have seen so many trainees do, which is to ignore the assessment requirements and then regret it when they receive their grades.
- Essay/assignment deadlines have been set for a reason. Although there is no doubt that these deadlines have been imposed to aid the smooth running of the assessment process, they are also there to help you. We all know that it is human nature to prevaricate and these deadlines have been imposed to avoid a log-jam of work for you at the end of the course.

For those of you for whom essay/assignment writing is a problem, we have provided further detailed guidance for you below. Hopefully the somewhat formulaic approach will provide sufficient support to allow you to find a stress-free route through the academic elements of your course.

Producing an essay or an assignment

The first thing to make absolutely clear is that there is no one definitive method for writing an essay or assignment. However, although lecturers, trainers and tutors all have their different styles, they will still be looking to see whether you have adhered to the general principles of writing an academic paper. Most academics would, therefore, accept that there are four main stages involved in developing an assignment.

The research stage

In this stage you need to find out the essential information required for the assignment. Whether you have a choice about the assignment topic, or whether it is a compulsory focus, the title or question should provide you with a clue as to the context and content of the paper. Ensure that you read widely around the subject, and that you support your work with a balance of texts and websites. Make sure, also, that you select sources that are contemporary, especially when you are writing about issues and topics where scenarios and viewpoints are constantly changing. Support your work with a range of literature on the topic, and do not rely too much on specific texts. Educational newspapers and magazines and Department for Children, Families and Schools (DCFS) documents will all provide alternative viewpoints for you to consider. It is fine to use the internet to source your paper, but make sure you only use reputable websites. Wikipedia, for example, is not recognized as an acceptable source for academic assignments. You are strongly advised to keep organized and efficient notes to support your reading. Using a highlighter pen to identify relevant sections of your notes is an effective way to identify information for your paper.

The planning stage

It is very important not to underestimate the value of planning your paper. Bearing in mind your heavy workload, it is understandable that you simply want to get your assignment out of the way as quickly as possible. However, rushing the process will only result in you having to re-do your work at a later stage. Hopefully, if your planning is of a good standard, it will provide you with a transparent and painless journey through the writing process. Giving yourself adequate planning time will help you to organize the key aspects of your assignment and then break these down into sub-categories. At this stage, you need to draft any specific arguments and debates you want to discuss, and make a note as to how you are going to support these with potential texts or references. You are highly likely to be given a word limit for the assignment, so you need to consider a word-count for each of the sections. You also need to give some consideration to the time you intend to allocate to each section and to the essay in general.

The reading and organization stage

You need to remember that not everything you have read will be relevant to your title, so make sure that you are ruthless in selecting those areas of text which reflect the content of your assignment. When trawling through literature, it is often a good idea to put sticky notes on those sections which you think might prove relevant later on. For those trainees who find it difficult to organize their material in a coherent manner, the following strategy might be useful. Try photocopying various sections of text, cutting these up and placing them into one of your three sections of 'Introduction', 'Core' and 'Conclusion'. Although this may appear to be a rather circuitous approach, it does cater for the kinaesthetic and visual learners who need physically to produce a framework for their assignment before they start writing. Some trainees like to use mind maps to organize ideas. You can then add more and more detail to these, and order them when you are ready.

The writing stage

It is at this stage that you need to prepare a first draft of your paper. Many people find it hard actually to begin to write on a blank piece of paper. Just write – anything – even if it is nonsense, and eventually the rest will come. With the ease of word-processing, you can cut and paste very simply. However, you must remember that this is only a first effort, and it is inevitable that you will have to review and revise it. You may need to be quite ruthless, especially if you are significantly over your word-count. When editing your work, cut or revise long-winded passages, avoid clichés and slang, and don't waffle. The message is simple: if the text does not relate to the essay/assignment title in some way then ditch it.

We cannot stress the importance of the proofreading process. This too needs to be carried out in stages. Check your assignment through very carefully by reading your work out loud as though to a public audience. By doing this, you will be able to recognize where to put commas and full stops. If you find it hard to read aloud, the chances are that your tutor will find it hard to read. You also need to check very carefully for poor punctuation, grammar and spelling. When checking spellings, don't rely entirely on a computer spellchecker as it may not pick up typos, for example 'form' instead of 'from'. You need to bear in mind that an assignment that is poorly written, and which contains spelling and grammatical errors, is likely to receive poor marks even if your ideas are excellent. The other question you need to ask yourself is 'Does the work flow?' Does it follow a logical sequence, or have you jumped from one idea to another? In hindsight, do you think that everything has been adequately explained? Finally, check your conclusion through to see whether you have inadvertently slipped any new ideas into this section.

The second stage requires you to get someone else to read through your assignment. You could ask a teacher to do this, as he or she is likely to be well versed in current educational issues. You may be able to ask your mentor or professional tutor who has probably had a great deal of experience in proofreading and editing trainee assignments.

The structure

A good assignment needs to have a clear structure with a well-thought-out introductory section.

This is your opportunity to provide a contextual background to your assignment and to set the scene. You need to explain the purpose of your assignment, for example what you are going to be discussing and/or debating, and the specific areas of interest. This introductory section is also the place to outline your assignment journey. The main section should have a clear structure and should demonstrate your knowledge of theory. Most courses will require you to analyse source literature critically and put forward your own ideas and opinions. Make sure you reference material properly using the Harvard System (the system used in this book). Keep reading the assessment criteria for the assignment to keep you on track. The conclusion should draw together all the threads discussed in the main section. It might summarize your findings and thoughts and offer ways forward.

Appropriate style

Find out what style is required of you. For example, are you expected to write in the first person? Try to see your 'audience' as people with intelligence who have a reasonable grasp of the subject matter but who are not necessarily experts. Do not make assumptions and try to make your points as explicit as possible.

Good presentation

Each training provider will have its own protocol in terms of the way you are expected to present your essay/assignments. However, as a rule, these are usually expected to be word-processed with the final draft in double-line spacing. All pages should be numbered appropriately and you should make good use of 'headers and footers'.

Providers usually like your work to be presented in an appropriate plastic presentation folder rather than in a lever-arch file, as these tend to be bulky. However, find out exactly what is required. You could present your work using the following layout:

- a front sheet which specifies your assignment title, your name, the date and word-count
- the assignment
- bibliography
- appendixes if relevant.

Arguments or ideas that are supported by evidence

When writing your essay/assignment, you need to be very cautious in your assertions. It is very important that you write with clarity and relevance, and that you only make claims which you can substantiate either with quotations or with other evidence. The aim of your paper will be to produce and present a series of coherent arguments that offer alternative viewpoints on the issue in question. When giving the 'for/against', 'pros/cons', 'strengths/weaknesses' of the issue, you need to identify and use relevant texts to support these viewpoints. Of course, you can express your own views, but you need to support these by citing the work of published authors who share your premise. Academic writing should take on an exploratory stance, should be 'open-minded' and should recognize that there will always be people who do not share your particular viewpoint on the issues in question.

Referencing your essays/assignments

At this level, you need to be able to reference your work in accordance with the Harvard protocol. This guidance has also been reproduced with the kind permission of the Norfolk and Suffolk SCITT training provider.

Harvard referencing guide

Referencing is important because it helps those people who read or mark your work to identify, locate and read the sources you have used. The Harvard referencing system is one of the main methods used for this purpose.

References should be cited twice in your assignment: first, at the point at which the source is referred to in your text; second, in an alphabetical reference list (or bibliography) at the end of your assignment.

Additional reading that you have not quoted from directly may also be incorporated into the bibliography.

Using references within the text of your paper

You should incorporate cited publications into the body of your assignment as follows:

In a recent article Smithson (1998) reports that …

According to James et al. (1993) … (Note use of 'et al.' (meaning 'and others') when there are three or more authors.)

Quotations

Page references should be given for all quotations. Avoid excessive use of word-for-word quotations. If a quotation is no more than three lines, it may be incorporated in the body of the text in quotation marks. For example Burnard (1992) asserts that 'As people begin to disclose themselves to other people, their rate of talking often speeds up. Thoughts run into one another and are made into sentences.'

If the quotation is longer, it must be entered as an extract and indented from the main text. It is not necessary to use quotation marks. For example Dixie (2007, p. 106) states that

> It is your role as a teacher to educate children to take responsibility for their own behaviour in your classes. Any attempt to 'over control' children in the classroom, without giving them an opportunity to take responsibility for their actions, is simply doomed to fail. If you exercise authoritarian control over your children without giving them the opportunity to make and learn from their mistakes, then you are well on course for conflict with them.

Summarizing in your own words

If you summarize in your own words what someone else has said, you should acknowledge the original author and provide the date of the publication in the text of your work. For example, 'As a group, females tend to be more successful than males (Argyle, 1988), and this ...' Please note that it may not be possible to supply a page reference if you are summarizing a chapter or larger section of the work.

Citing secondary sources

Sometimes you may wish to cite a secondary source that refers to the original work (primary source) but which you may not have actually seen. Secondary sources should be cited in the following way:

> Those perceptions, which enter with most force and violence, we may name *impressions* ... By ideas I mean the faint images of these in thinking and reasoning ... (Hume, 1941, cited in Sartre, 1972, p. 2)

Edited works

When the quotation comes from an edited work, where each chapter has its own particular author, you should give details in your text of the author of the chapter, the publication date of the whole book and the page number(s) on which the quotation appears, for example:

> Nursing scientists in general are either interested in or pressurised into 'testing' theories empirically rather than 'evaluating' or 'reflecting' on what theories are being produced or how they are being produced. (Kim, 1989, p. 106)

This example is a quotation from a chapter written by Kim, but which appears in a book edited by J.A. Akinsanya. In the bibliography at the end of your assignment this would appear thus:

> Kim, H.S. (1989) Theoretical thinking in nursing: problems and prospects, in J.A. Akinsanya (ed.), *Theories and Models of Nursing*. Edinburgh Churchill Livingstone.

The bibliography at the end of your assignment

At the end of your assignment you should organize your references alphabetically in one sequence by authors' surnames following the formats below.

Book references

To reference a book you need to note:

- the author/editor(s) surname(s) and initial(s)
- the date of publication of that edition (no reprint dates)
- title and subtitle of the work in italics
- edition of the book other than the first
- volume number if it is part of a multi-volume set
- and publisher place of publication.

Examples

Arts Council (1995) *Excellence in Schools*. London, HMSO.

Feldstein, R. et al. (eds) (1996) *Reading Seminars I and II: Lacan's Return to Freud*. New York, State University of New York [Use et al. when there are three or more authors.]

Knot, G. and Waites, N. (1988) *Computer Studies*. 4th ed. Sunderland Business Education Publishers:
[Include both authors when there are only two.]

Journal references

To reference a journal you need to know the following:

- author(s) surname and initial(s)

- year article was published
- title of the article
- title of the journal (in italics) containing the article
- volume number
- part number (in brackets). If the journal is a weekly publication, the actual date of the issue may be added
- page numbers.

Examples

Berry, M.J. and Vishnick, C. (1994) 'Counselling practice.' *Nursing Standard* 9(9), 33–36.

Cunningham, M. (1999) 'Saying sorry: the politics of apology.' *Political Quarterly* 70:(30), 285–293.

Internet references

As internet references are of an ephemeral nature, it is good practice to include a copy of the source of reference as an appendix to your assignment. You need to include the following:

- author/editor(s)
- year
- title of article in italics
- (online)
- (edition)
- place of publication
- publisher (if known)
- available from: use web address
- (date accessed).

Examples

Parra, L. (1999) *Information Ownership* (online). Available from: http:// humanism.org/~/ucas/ip/short.html (accessed 19 February 1999).

Student Grants and Loans: A brief guide for higher education students (online). Available from: http://www.open.gov.uk/dfee/loans/loans.htm (accessed 19 September 1998).

Online journal article references

- The citation order is as follows:
- author(s)

- year
- title of article
- title of journal (in italics) containing the article
- (online)
- volume (issue)
- pagination
- available from: use web address
- (date accessed).

Example

Haggard, P. (2001) 'The psychology of action.' *British Journal of Psychology* (online), 92(1), pp. 113–128, Available from: http://barbarina.catchword. com/vl=8356867/d=30/nw=1/rpsv/catchword (accessed 21 July 2001).

Email references

The citation order is as follows:

- sender
- (sender's email address)
- day, month, year
- subject of message (in italics)
- email to recipient
- (recipient's email address).

Example

Smith, A. (Asmith@hotmail.com) 7 August 2000. *RE: Canadian Rainfall*. Email to M. James (Mjames@suffolk.ac.uk).

16 Improving your subject knowledge for teaching

One of the biggest areas of concern for trainees is their perceived vulnerability as far as their level of subject knowledge is concerned. This is especially true of primary teachers who have to teach a diverse range of subjects to 11-year-olds. The main question that they tend to ask themselves is – is my subject knowledge good enough to effectively support the learning of children?

In this part of the book we intend to focus on these standards, namely Q14 and Q15, not only because of the great emphasis placed on subject knowledge and pedagogy by the TDA, but because experience has shown us that the quality of teaching and learning in a lesson is often directly related to the quality of the trainee's subject knowledge. These standards are presented below.

> Q14 Have a secure knowledge and understanding of their subjects/curriculum areas and related pedagogy to enable them to teach effectively across the age and ability range for which they are trained.

You will note that there are two requirements of the standard – you need to demonstrate a secure subject knowledge **and** related pedagogy. In other words you are not only required to prove that you have a solid fund of overt subject knowledge, but you also need to show that you know how to transform this so that children across the whole of the primary age-range can learn. This was first mentioned in Chapter 9. Very often trainees assume that they do not need as much subject knowledge to teach younger children. Then they realize that it is often harder to get their heads around the pedagogy involved. For example, they themselves have no problems telling the time, but they have no idea how to teach this to children. They are not aware of children's misconceptions and errors, and wonder why children do not learn from them. If you have both overt subject knowledge and pedagogical knowledge, you will be able to

- plan individual lessons in an effective and challenging manner
- plan effective and challenging sequences of lessons and schemes of work

- set challenging teaching and learning objectives
- assess children's progress towards these objectives
- set subject-related targets for individuals and groups of children
- react confidently and accurately to children's questions
- successfully break down ideas and concepts and sequence them logically to support the development of children's knowledge and understanding
- recognize and respond to children's common misconceptions
- make effective interventions to construct and scaffold children's learning
- analyse children's progress and make accurate assessments of their learning and achievement
- critically reflect upon issues relating to this standard
- hold informed discussion with your tutors and colleagues
- produce effective essays and/or assignments on related issues.

The other standard which relates to subject knowledge is Q15 which states:

> Q15 Know and understand the relevant statutory and non-statutory curricula frameworks, including those provided through the national strategies, for their subjects/curriculum areas, and other relevant initiatives applicable to the age and ability range for which they are trained.

This requires you to gain a secure knowledge of the curricula frameworks within which you will be working. In effect, this means that you will need to demonstrate a knowledge and understanding of the relevant aspects of the National Curriculum, as set out in the National Curriculum handbook. You will need to demonstrate that you fully understand the three principles of inclusion: the need to set suitable learning challenges; the need to respond to children's diverse needs; and the need to find ways to overcome barriers to learning and assessment for individuals and groups. You will need to reflect your understanding of these principles in your lesson-planning and teaching. You are also required to know about and understand the principles and approaches to teaching underpinning the primary national strategy, including the Literacy and Numeracy Frameworks. You will also be expected to have a knowledge and understanding of the Key Stage 1 and 2 National Curriculum programmes of study and the Early Years Foundation Stage Curriculum if relevant.

You can show your competence in this area by demonstrating your ability to

- make reference to the relevant curricula, frameworks and initiatives in your planning
- plan for and practise inclusion in your lessons

- show your knowledge and understanding of national strategy approaches in your planning and teaching
- critically reflect upon issues relating to this standard
- hold informed discussions with your tutors and colleagues
- produce effective essays and/or assignments on related issues.

Just as you would expect to monitor the progress and achievement of the children in your classes, so the TDA requires its training providers to monitor your subject and pedagogical knowledge over the training period. Training providers have been asked to audit your subject/ pedagogical knowledge at the beginning of the course, and to monitor your progress in this field throughout your training. It is up to you, therefore, to make sure that you provide evidence to illustrate this progress. Different training providers use different methods to do this, some of which are described below.

Some training providers require their trainees to 'traffic-light' their subject knowledge at the beginning of the course. Trainees are asked to highlight the various elements of the National Curriculum or examination syllabuses in one of three colours: green, to show their *confidence in being able to teach* this element of subject knowledge; amber, if they are only partially confident *of their ability to deliver* this aspect of the curriculum; and red, if their subject knowledge is rusty or non-existent and if they *do not feel confident in being able to deliver* this to their children. This highlighted document is then presented to the mentor/tutor before the trainee starts to teach. Please note the emphasis being placed on your confidence levels in *being able to teach* the specific elements of the curriculum. Simply knowing your subject is not enough; you must be able to deliver this content effectively to your children. How this subject knowledge is tracked varies across providers. Some providers issue these audits on a regular basis and ask trainees to complete them periodically; in this way progress can be plotted. Other providers are quite happy for trainees simply to add annotated notes alongside the highlighted text.

Some providers require their trainees to keep a weekly 'subject knowledge for teaching' audit-tracking sheet, on which they are required to log all the things they have done to improve this aspect of their teaching. This log is then verified by the subject tutor and/or the professional tutor on a regular basis. Trainees are required to make reference to any new subject knowledge they have picked up while on courses, when researching and planning their lessons, when observing colleagues and while researching essays and assignments.

If your training provider has not been prescriptive in how you demonstrate your progress in these two standards, then you need to come up with your own strategies for plotting your journey. As Graduate Teacher external mentors, one of the questions we ask every time we meet with our trainees is – what evidence do you have to show that you have developed your subject and pedagogical knowledge since the time of my last visit? If they cannot demonstrate progress here, we will not sign these standards off. If you have not been given guidance on how to plot your progress with subject knowledge for teaching, the example in Table 16.1 may help you to do this.

Table 16.1 An effective way to record your subject knowledge for teaching

Task/experience	How this has supported my subject knowledge for teaching
I have read through the NC programmes of study for art; my school's policy; school medium-term plans and the Suffolk Art document. After our art lectures, I have made copious notes and further researched specific artists. I have watched teachers' TV clips of primary teachers teaching art. I visited a nearby school which had just run an art week. I have looked at children's sketchbooks throughout the school to see what expectations I should have.	I have been team teaching a Year 6 class with my mentor. I have made notes and kept examples of children's work. This has enabled me to see what I should expect of Year 6. I have taught the final two lessons of the unit myself and used my research on Van Gogh to help me plan. I was clear about what children in Year 5 could do, through looking at their sketchbooks, and this helped me set the Year 6 children appropriate targets and provide them with challenging feedback. I displayed their work in an innovative way having seen examples of this at the neighbouring school. I just felt so confident in what to teach, how to teach it, what expectations to have and how to move the children forward. It was brilliant. Without the subject knowledge, I would have floundered.

Bearing in mind the large numbers of ITT providers in the country, it has obviously not been possible to provide you with programme-specific guidance on the issue of subject knowledge for teaching. If you require this level of detail, you will need to explore the literature and website pages of the relevant ITT provider/programme. Having said this, we hope you feel that the advice proffered in this chapter has gone some way to helping you to meet the generalized requirements that would be expected in any ITT course.

Part Six
UNDERSTANDING YOUR SCHOOL PRACTICES

Different types of school practices 17

Let's face it – this is probably the moment you have all been waiting for. Walking through the gates of your first teaching practice school is something you probably envisaged from the time you first started to think about teaching as a potential career. There is also no doubt about the momentous nature of the occasion, as your experiences in your practice schools are likely to impact heavily upon you as a person and as a professional for the rest of your life. It is also no exaggeration to say that the experiences you are about to embark upon represent an extremely steep learning curve, and that there will be times when you are bound to feel that you are simply 'not up to the job'. Most trainees feel this at some stage in their placements, as there is an overwhelming amount of information to take on board, and a daunting number of new skills to learn.

Every trainee will undertake a different learning experience. You will all be placed in totally different schools for your practices, and will meet and learn from a variety of professionals. Your provider will try to place you in contrasting schools so that you experience different approaches, catchment areas and ways of working. A placement in a large urban school is very different from learning in a small village school with three teachers. Not only will you learn different things in each school, but this will also give you the opportunity to decide what kind of school you eventually want to teach in.

The next few chapters have been written with a full understanding of the intricacies of the journey ahead, and will hopefully guide you through the complex and challenging process of learning to teach. Although we have provided you with a pretty comprehensive set of guidance and advice on how to succeed as a trainee teacher, there really is no substitute for learning from your mistakes.

18 Acclimatizing yourself to the school

Once you know the name of your first practice school you need to do everything you can to prepare for your experience. One of the first things to do is to phone the school and ask for a school prospectus to be sent to you. Reading through this will provide an understanding of how your training fits into a specific school context. The prospectus will provide contextual information on the demographic, socio-economic and academic make-up of the school and will help to prepare you for the type of children you will be teaching. To support this process, it would be useful to log on to the school website and access as much information as possible about the school. Often a brief drive around the school's catchment area will give you a rough idea of the type of children you can expect to be teaching, although it is important to note that many schools have large numbers of children from outside their catchment area. Most websites and brochures contain abridged versions of the school's latest Ofsted report which you can use to find out more about the school. If it is a fairly recent report, you will be able to get a feel for the school's current strengths and priorities.

You may have the opportunity to visit the school prior to your placement. This is a good opportunity for you to get to know the colleagues you will be working with, and for them to find out more about you. If possible, spend some time observing your mentor teach, and familiarize yourself with the classroom in which you will be working. If possible, ask for copies of key policy documents such as those relating to behaviour management, teaching and learning, assessment and child protection/safeguarding. Reading through these ahead of your placement can really give you an understanding of how the school works, and of the practices you will have to accommodate.

It is important that you make the right impression during these initial meetings. The staff want to know that you are enthusiastic and keen, but be careful not to bombard them with questions and requests for documents. They are very busy people, and it is important to ask for things at appropriate times.

A cautionary note

Before you start your school practice you need to be well aware of the health and safety issues that are likely to confront you during your training. In short, you need to know how to protect yourself.

- Make sure you never leave children unattended when you have sole responsibility for the class.
- When teaching PE or other practical subjects which involve hazardous tools or equipment, make sure your mentor is present and helps you check health and safety requirements.
- Make sure you follow the school's policy for child protection and safeguarding, and report anything you are concerned about to the appropriate member of staff.
- There are limited circumstances when appropriate physical restraint may be used with children, but make sure you understand fully what your individual school's policy is in this area. As a general rule physical contact with children is to be avoided.
- Although it is highly unlikely, you do need to know that it is possible that a child could make an accusation of abuse against you while you are on teaching practice. The advice is simple: avoid being alone with a child. If you have to talk to a child privately, inform a nearby colleague and leave the door open so that you are both in full view.

Our advice to you would also be to join the students' section of a teachers' union or professional association and to extend this when you enter the profession as an NQT. Usually membership is free for trainees and some unions will even give you a reduced membership rate when you start your induction year.

Some of you may be fortunate enough to be placed in schools with one or more fellow trainees, which will make the whole process less daunting. However, if you are on your own, your colleagues on your course can still prove to be an invaluable form of moral and practical support. You need to take time and opportunity to share resources, to explore ideas and discuss your vulnerabilities. Talk to each other via email or your course's virtual-learning environment. This is not the time to be competitive – there is room for more than one brilliant trainee on the course!

19 Preparing yourself psychologically for your practice

Be prepared for periods of extreme self-doubt during your teaching practices. However, whenever you simply feel like giving up, remember that you will either be moving practice schools soon, or starting as an NQT at some point in the near future. Take it from us, it does not get any harder than when you are on your teaching practices. Having to meet the many and varied demands of the school and the training programme, while at the same time planning meaningful and stimulating lessons for your children, is difficult. It would, therefore, be extremely surprising if you did not question whether you really want to teach and/or whether you are any good at the job. Try to remind yourself that when you are in your own school with your own classes, it **will** become easier. You also need to hold on to the fact that every teacher trainee across the country is feeling, or has felt, the same as you at some point during their training. This is why it is so important to talk openly to fellow trainees about some of the issues troubling you. However, having said this, if you feel that the pressures of meeting your training and teaching demands are beginning to have an adverse effect on your health and on your ability to make sound judgements, you need to speak to your tutor about this.

Dealing with stress

You will have gathered from reading the above text that stress could be a major issue while you are on your teaching practices. We all need a degree of stress in order to perform well, but there is a limit to how much we can tolerate. You are highly likely to find yourself feeling stressed in school-based situations where you are:

- unable to meet your assignment deadlines
- anxious about meeting the required standards of the course
- worried about managing the behaviour of particularly difficult children
- in a school that does not provide you with enough support
- struggling to keep up with the workload.

When asked about what causes stress, many people put this down to simply having too much work to do. It is not as simple as this. Stress is not necessarily caused by the amount of work we have got to do, but is often more down to a lack of control and ownership of the tasks being given to us. It is important that you make yourself fully aware of the potential signs of stress so that you can nip these in the bud. Signs of stress could be:

- frequent headaches
- exhaustion
- insomnia
- a feeling of powerlessness and lack of control
- panic attacks
- crying at inappropriate times
- feeling inadequate and depressed.

If you will accept the premise that stress is caused by a feeling of impotence and a lack of control over your workload, then you will be receptive to the fact that there will be things you can do to improve your situation. Here are some suggestions.

- Improving your time management is absolutely crucial. If you have an essay or an assignment to do, you need to consult your calendar in order to give yourself plenty of time to plan and complete it. Start assignments early if you can – this will help you access resources and gather any practical information you need. Look ahead to lessons you have to plan for the future to give yourself time to gather resources and gain the necessary subject knowledge.
- Make sure you keep up to date with paperwork. Plan in time to collect evidence for your portfolio. Evaluate your lessons straight after you teach them if you can. File plans and resources so you know where they are.
- You also need to build 'checking' and 'amending' time into your planning. You should show your planning to your mentor to check it over. It is only reasonable that you give him or her at least a couple of days to do this. This is particularly important at the start of your practice when you are beginning to get to know the abilities of the children, and need to be sure you have pitched your lesson at the right level.
- Before you leave school each day make sure that you have a pretty good idea of what you will be teaching the next day. This ensures you will have checked out resources.
- Plan your week carefully. If you are a morning person, go to bed early, get a good night's sleep, get into school early and do the bulk of your preparation and/or marking then. Conversely, if you work better at the end of the day, stay on at school and get your work done then.

- Make sure that you plan some leisure-time activities into your week.
- You cannot possibly do everything perfectly. Learn to prioritize and don't get diverted by interesting but futile side issues.
- If you feel that you are suffering from stress, you need to seek medical help and inform your tutor. They would prefer to know early on if you are finding things difficult rather than hear about you experiencing significant difficulties which might call into question your ability to finish the course.
- Understand that all your feedback will help you develop. There will always be things you can improve on. Treat the feedback you receive during your school practices as preparation for your teaching, and not merely as a means to gain a good teaching-practice grade. Be prepared to experiment. If things go wrong it does not really matter as no one will be expecting you to get everything right. Even if a lesson goes completely awry, with the right approach you will be able to learn something from the experience. Adopting a more sanguine approach to making mistakes will go a long way to reducing your stress levels.
- Be both proactive and reflective in your training. Your mentor will really appreciate you coming to the table with a balanced evaluation of your progress and/or lesson. By doing this you will be able to exercise some control over the feedback process.
- Make good use of your planning, preparation and assessment (PPA) time in school. Make sure you know what you are going to do in that time, and make sure you get it done. We all work harder and better when we work to time-limits.

Understanding your development as a trainee

20

One of the things that can help you to take a balanced and informed view of your teaching-practice experiences is to understand your development as a trainee teacher over the year. Numerous studies carried out into ITT/induction issues reveal that there is a high degree of predictability in the attitudes, emotions and behaviours exhibited by trainees at specific points along the training continuum. As you can see from the model provided in Figure 20.1 (Furlong and Maynard, 1995), most trainees enter their training with a fairly idealistic view of teaching. They firmly believe that, provided they treat their children with reasonableness and respect, this approach will be immediately reciprocated. However, what these trainees initially fail to understand is that teaching and learning relationships are far more complex than this and that there is a great deal of hard work to do in order to win over the trust of their children. Once they understand this, they recognize the need for a more robust approach towards behaviour management and begin to search for the strategies that will help them simply to survive in the classroom.

You need to understand that because this realization has the effect of stripping away some of your ideals, this can be an extremely emotional part of your training. Some trainees, once their behaviour management and planning is of a reasonable standard, start to coast for the rest of their practice. You will see from the model presented in Figure 20.1 that the role of the mentor also changes in response to the changing needs of the trainee. Any mentor worth their salt who recognizes that you are not making the progress you should be making, will simply do everything he or she can to move you off the plateau. Be prepared for this to be an uncomfortable experience.

Figure 20.1 is a developmental model showing you that many of the feelings and emotions experienced at specific points in your training are predictable and will pass. This is not to say that all trainees will progress at exactly the same pace. Some, for example, will spend far longer in the survival stage than others. However, it is worth noting that the training journey is fairly predictable and that you will get through it.

Early idealism	Survival	Hitting a plateau	Moving on
'I'm a reasonable and caring person – I am sure that if I show this side of me, my children will respect me. On this basis I am confident that I can get through to them.'	'Help! I'm going under! On its own this approach is not working. I now realize that I need to be stronger in establishing, maintaining and reinforcing my expectations, rules, rewards and sanctions in a warm, caring but nevertheless assertive and consistent manner.'	'Generally speaking I've got my behaviour management sorted. The kids aren't rioting so I can relax now, knowing that I have got this teaching thing taped. I'll start pushing myself in my NQT year.'	'My mentor seems to want blood! He doesn't seem to be happy with what I am doing at the moment and is constantly setting me targets.'

TRAINER   →   CRITICAL FRIEND   →   CO-ENQUIRER

Note the changing role of the subject mentor as you progress through the year.

Figure 20.1 Understanding the developmental nature of your training (adapted from Furlong and Maynard, 1995)

It is important to remember that your tutor and mentor will be keen for you to do as well as you can in your practices, and reach the highest grades possible for your teaching. Everyone will be setting you targets to help you move from 'satisfactory' to 'good', or from 'good' to 'very good'.

Understanding the roles of those supporting the training process

21

The external tutor

Each trainee will be assigned an external tutor who will liaise with the trainee and the school. The external tutor understands the organization and content of their specific ITT programme, and, when visiting you in school, should offer you and the school mentor the support you need to realize your QTS standards.

The external tutor also meets with the ITT tutor or professional tutor in the school to ensure that all parties have the necessary support required for them to meet their training responsibilities. It is also their responsibility to check that the training programme is being properly implemented by the school, and to make sure that trainees are receiving the support they need from relevant training staff.

The school

Before you start your teaching practices you need to understand that your school will play a major role in your training and in your assessment against the standards for QTS. This process will be overseen by an ITT tutor or professional tutor whom you may or may not get to see on a regular basis. Quite often this will be the headteacher. The school will also assign you to a mentor who will have responsibility for working closely with you and will guide you on issues relating to your planning, assessment, teaching and learning. This mentor will have ultimate responsibility for the classes you teach and should meet with you regularly, at least once a week, in a designated time-slot to review your progress. The mentor will also support you in maintaining a training file or school-practice folder and in compiling your portfolio of evidence. Your mentor will undertake regular formal and informal observations, and provide you with verbal and written feedback identifying both your strengths and areas for improvement. Through the medium of meaningful discussion, observation and demonstration, she will provide opportunities for you to learn and improve your professional practice.

When supporting you, your mentor should make continual reference to the standards for QTS and help you to achieve competence in these and identify evidence which demonstrates exactly how these standards are being met.

Professional tutor

Your professional tutor should oversee your training and progress throughout your placement. She should talk to your mentor regularly about your training and ensure that the whole school community is involved in this. She should ensure that your weekly meetings are occurring and that you have been observed and given feedback.

Mentor

You should expect your mentor to:

- provide opportunities for you to improve your subject knowledge for teaching
- offer you advice and guidance on how to develop your planning, assessment, teaching and classroom-management skills
- hold regular weekly meetings with you and ensure that the agreed key points and targets in the meeting are recorded
- make regular lesson observations and provide you with verbal and written feedback
- help you access other training you may need with the help of other members of staff in the school
- assess your professional practice against the standards for QTS and moderate this assessment with both your professional tutor and external tutor. This may include 'signing off' pieces of evidence in your portfolio.
- complete the relevant assessment paperwork required by your training provider.

When you undertake your first practice you might find it difficult to be objective about your experiences. In other words, you simply 'don't know what you don't know'. By providing you with a list of your training entitlements we hope that you will be able to ascertain whether any aspects of your training are missing. If, having read this chapter, you feel that you have cause for complaint then you need make contact with your external tutor in order to discuss the situation.

Interacting positively with other members of staff

Teaching is very much a team-game and there is absolutely no place for the lone wolf. It is vital to establish and cultivate good professional relationships with all of your colleagues if you are going to do the very best for your children. Knowing how to act in a professional manner and how to cultivate good collaborative relationships are deemed to be very important by the TDA, who devote specific QTS standards to this issue. These are outlined below:

> Q4 Communicate effectively with children, young people, colleagues, parents and carers.
>
> Q5 Recognize and respect the contribution that colleagues, parents and carers can make to the development and well-being of children and young people and to raising their achievement.
>
> Q20 Know and understand the roles of colleagues with specific responsibilities, including those with responsibility for learners with special educational needs or disabilities and other learning needs.
>
> Q32 Work as team member and identify opportunities for working with colleagues, sharing the development of effective practice with them.
>
> Q33 Ensure that colleagues working with them are appropriately involved in supporting learning and understand the roles they are expected to fulfil.

Imperative as it is for you to gain competence in these standards as a means of obtaining your QTS award, they are fundamentally much more important than this. The quality of your relationships lies at the very heart of your interaction with the people with whom you work on a daily basis, and your competence in realizing these standards can often be displayed through the quality of your verbal and non-verbal communication. A brief guide is provided below to help you to get off on the right foot with those working closest to you.

Working with your external tutor

- Try to remember that irrespective of their seniority in the training pecking order, this person is a guest in the school and, as such, should be treated with courtesy and respect. Find him an appropriate space in which to meet with you and your mentor, and make sure that you offer refreshments during his visit. Do not forget that he may be unfamiliar with the timings of your school day, so ensure that he is aware of lesson start-times and break-times, and so on.

- If there is a mismatch between the requirements of the training provider and the needs of the school, then take the opportunity to discuss this with your tutor. Whatever happens, do not try to solve the issue all by yourself.
- If your tutor intends to observe you, then make sure that you provide him with a detailed lesson plan and a context sheet outlining details of any teaching/learning-related issues that may inform the observation. Be extremely receptive to the feedback offered and ask for ways in which you can put this advice into practice.
- Make sure that you are fully organized and prepared for his visit. Have all the relevant paperwork to hand.
- If you are not sure about anything, do not leave it – ask.

Working with your mentor

Your mentor is the most important person in your school life, so it is worth doing everything you can to cultivate and maintain good professional relationships with her. Remember that first impressions are very difficult to change. Arrive for your first day on time and show that you are well prepared. Show willingness to learn and enthusiasm for teaching in general and demonstrate an understanding and empathy for her demanding workload.

- Find out about the practical issues such as photocopying and resources and whether you are expected to attend meetings and assemblies. Ask about the specific customs of your school. Whom do you have to pay for tea, coffee and lunches? Make sure you find out about, and adhere to, the staff dress-code.
- It is very important to remember that the role of mentor is voluntary and that, although some of them might receive some time off to carry out their role, they are never fully compensated for all their hard work. Having said this, they have committed themselves to certain responsibilities as far as your training is concerned, so they may need a gentle nudge from time to time.
- If you feel you really cannot manage a challenging child without your mentor's help, then simply say so.
- Ask if you can get involved with parents' evenings by sitting in on the interviews. In case you are invited to make a contribution, have a few notes on each child already prepared.

Working with other colleagues

- Try to engender really positive relationships with all whom you work with. Difficult as it will be at times, endeavour to stay cheerful and offer to help them with extra tasks. Having said this, you need to be very wary that you are not bombarded with an unrealistic amount of extra work. It is one thing to offer to help dress children for the school play, but quite another to be given the role of making all the costumes!
- Arrive early at the school on a daily basis if you can – not only does this show everyone that you are keen, but it gives you ample time to deal with any unforeseen circumstances that may arise. There will always be resources that you cannot find, or an interactive whiteboard that won't work!
- Attend some extra-curricular activities such as educational, fund-raising or social events. Not only will this impress your fellow colleagues but it will certainly get your children on board. It will also help you meet some of the standards.
- Although honesty is usually deemed to be the best policy, there will be times when you may have to curb your tongue. Even if it is obvious to you that your views and ideas are likely to improve the smooth running of the school, you need to remember that you have only just started your teaching career and that this is a time when you need to show some humility. There will be plenty of time for you to share your ideas once you have qualified.
- **Never** allow yourself to be embroiled in staffroom politics. Rest assured that any indiscreet slip of the tongue you make will spread like wildfire across the school, and you will spend a lot of time and energy trying to put things right.

22 Making effective use of classroom teaching assistants

It is highly likely that at some point during your teaching practices, you will be working with a TA (teaching assistant) or LSA (learning support assistant). For the purposes of this book, an additional adult in the classroom will be referred to as a TA. Bearing in mind that many of these colleagues are likely to have a far greater knowledge of the children and of the workings of the school in general than you, it is understandable that this might appear to be a potentially intimidating experience. In order to make the most of this working relationship and to rid this working arrangement of any ambiguities, it is important that you take control of the situation. Make sure you know exactly why the TA is in the classroom. Is he there to support one or two children or to provide more generalized support? Ascertain exactly what type of support he can offer the children.

It is always important to brief your TA, so he knows exactly what is required throughout the lesson. You can do this by talking to him beforehand, providing him with specific notes, or giving him a copy of your lesson plans which details what you want him to do. It is important that he does have a specific role at all stages of the lesson. TAs are there to support the learning of the children and, if they are not directed and fully utilized, they are a valuable resource that is being wasted. It is worth talking to your mentor about your TA's strengths and what he usually does. The sort of things TAs are expected to do are as follows:

- manage the behaviour of specific children
- help children to use the learning resources and equipment
- ensure that children fully understand instructions
- encourage participation by using the prompts and questions issued by the teacher
- rehearse answers with certain children ready for the plenary session
- remind children of set targets and help them to assess their own progress
- work with small groups and/or individuals
- extend and support the more able in the class

- support the least able in the class
- use an observation checklist to monitor participation
- scribe on the board while you are talking to the class
- undertake specific assessments.

Raise the status of your TA by ensuring that the children understand that you will be working as a team. It is important for you to show the class a united front and that you will not tolerate rudeness or lack of cooperation towards your colleague. Your mentor will have already established the extent of the role of the TA, and it is important that you follow this to avoid confusion. For example, if your mentor expects the TA to issue sanctions, then you should expect this too. When you have qualified, you will be able to set your own expectations of your TA. During the lesson, make sure you monitor all groups of children, including those your TA is working with. It is vital that you establish an overview of the whole class, and all children see you as 'teacher'. It is also important to meet with your TA after the lesson to evaluate how things went and to ask for his comments on the progress of the children with whom he was working.

23 Working with parents

It is highly unlikely that in your initial teaching practice(s) you will be expected to play a dominant role in communicating with parents. At this stage of your teaching career, unless your mentor is absent, your contribution will probably be reduced to a 'shadowing' and/or supportive role. However, by the time you reach your final practice, you could very well be asked to make a significant contribution to daily communication with parents and take a joint role in parents' evenings. We know from having discussed this issue with many trainees that this can be a time of potential anxiety.

At the beginning of your practice it would be worthwhile going into to the playground to listen to conversations between your mentor and some of the parents. Get a feel for how your mentor responds sensitively to their concerns and also tackles some of the more difficult issues such as problems with a particular child's behaviour. Talk to your mentor about the way to approach these issues and rehearse how you would do it. As time goes on and your mentor feels you are ready, have a go at talking to some of the parents together, and then on your own with your mentor listening.

As far as parents' evenings are concerned, it will be useful to attend one as soon as you can to observe your mentor. The purpose of consulting with parents is to nurture the home-school partnership and to use this relationship ultimately to improve teaching and learning. In particular look for the way your mentor enters into a dialogue with the parents so that both parties have an opportunity to contribute to the meeting. It is important for you as a teacher to learn as much as you can about a particular child so that you can personalize the learning as much as possible. It is also vital that parents know how their children are progressing; what the child's targets are; and how they can support their child at home. It will be useful for you to note the way your mentor prepares for this event: what paperwork/children's work is used; how difficult issues are tackled; and what records are kept. Below we have provided some top tips for parents' evenings.

Preparation is all!

Find out exactly who is coming to see you. Bearing in mind the high rate of marriage breakdown, it is almost inevitable that you will be meeting partners, step-parents, grandparents and other relatives.

- Find out from more experienced staff if any of the parents you are seeing can be difficult – and the best way to deal with them.
- Prepare notes on each of the children you teach and support this with their prior attainment data.
- If possible, check back to the child's previous report – it is embarrassing if your comments are very different from what has been said before – unless you have firm evidence to support this change of stance.
- Post a list of appointment times in a visible place. If parents are aware that there are others waiting, they will be more ready to stick to the schedule. Try to stick to the allocated time-slot.
- See if you can predict the issues that might arise and prepare some answers.
- Try to look confident even if you do not feel it. Remember, most parents will be nervous too.

Suggested structure

Introduction: 'Hello you must be X's mum', or 'You've come to talk about X' (don't use a surname unless you're sure of it, can pronounce it and know his or her title).

Headline: for example, 'X has settled in well and is making good progress.'

Strengths (social and academic): 'I'm particularly pleased with … (have a clear example to illustrate your point).

Areas for improvement (social and academic): 'However, X still needs to work on … (again, have some illustrations).

Parents' views: 'How do you feel that things are going? Do you have any worries?' (Make a note of their concerns.) If this discussion goes on for too long, say something like 'Can I suggest that we make another appointment to discuss this? I'm afraid there are a lot of people waiting.' If you are worried about the possible nature of this further meeting, discuss your concerns with your mentor, who will be able to offer you advice and support.

Parental help: 'Could you make sure that X practises …'?

Conclusion: Look at your watch, smile, stand up and offer a handshake. 'Well thank you very much for coming; it was good to meet you.'

Further tips

- Remember that parents want to know that you care about their child. Put their minds at ease by saying something positive about the child.
- Always try to be objective. Make sure you separate the work ethic and/ or behaviour from the child's personality. You are more likely to get somewhere if you offer your criticism in a warm and affirming manner.
- Keep a clock or watch on the table – try to be politely ruthless; a slight delay may lead to massive backlogs!
- Have a notebook in which to record the things that you promise to do. If you have said you will follow up on an issue, then make sure that you do.
- Develop your listening skills by allowing parents to have their full say. Many problems arise because of parents' frustrations that they are simply not being listened to. Do not get defensive and do not bear a grudge. You have to show them that you are better than this!
- Do not be afraid to ask for advice or support from colleagues during the evening if you need it.
- Use your experiences in dealing with challenging parents as learning opportunities. If you feel that you did not do yourself justice in your meeting, then ask the simple question, 'What would I do differently next time?'
- Celebrate your success when it's over!

Getting to grips with behaviour management

Behaviour management is an absolute priority for the majority of trainees in schools. It is this belief that has led Gererd to writing *Managing Your Classroom* (2007) which provides advice and guidance on how to establish and maintain an effective behaviour-management regime in your lessons. Because good behaviour management lies at the heart of effective teaching, it is absolutely vital that you either carry out some background reading into this issue (see the above book and the reading list provided in Chapter 4).

To support your reading on this issue further you should reflect on your pre-course observation data as discussed in Chapter 3. Chapter 4 also provides detailed advice on the link between body language and assertive discipline. So important is behaviour management to the classroom practitioner that the TDA has allocated a total of four standards to this issue. These are as follows:

Q1 Have high expectations of children and young people including a commitment to ensuring that they can achieve their full educational potential and to establishing fair, respectful, trusting, supportive and constructive relationships with them.

Q10 Have a knowledge and understanding of a range of teaching, learning and behaviour management strategies and know how to use and adapt them, including how to personalise learning and provide opportunities for all learners to achieve their potential.

Q30 Establish a purposeful and safe learning environment conducive to learning and identify opportunities for learners to learn in out of school contexts.

Q31 Establish a clear framework for classroom discipline to manage learners' behaviour constructively and promote their self-control and independence.

If you are working with a class that has some children with extremely challenging behaviour, then you need to speak to your tutor about this. It is unrealistic to expect a trainee teacher such as yourself to cope with these children all the time. Having said this, it is fair to say that you are likely to come across some extremely challenging behaviour from time to time in your lessons, so you need to be prepared to deal with this. Although it is unrealistic to expect you to become a proficient behaviour-manager overnight, there are a number of things you can do to reduce the opportunities for children to disrupt your lessons. As you will see below, this advice fits into two distinct categories: those relating to whole-class behaviour-management planning and those linked to your relationship issues with children.

Whole-class behaviour-management planning (Technical Domain)

- Make sure you have read your placement school's behaviour policy and that you are clear about the class routines, rules, rewards and sanctions. It will be necessary for you to follow the same systems with the class as your mentor, and to have the same expectations, otherwise the children will become confused.
- Make sure that you constantly revisit your rules, routines, rewards and sanctions with your class on a regular basis and that you issue your sanctions and rewards in a **consistent** manner. You could do this in the following way: 'I want you to watch me demonstrate this, then I want you to think of some questions you would like to ask. What are our rules for this? Remember if you don't put your hand up, I will write your name on the board.'
- Make sure that the work is set at the appropriate level for each child in the class. Provide opportunities for differentiation by task, resource, outcome, questioning and preferred learning styles. Because you will not know the children very well in the early stages of your practice, this will be difficult to achieve. However, as you get to know your children, you will get to know their strengths and 'areas for development' and it will become much easier to offer them opportunities for personalized learning. If children are fully challenged and engaged in their work, they are less likely to misbehave.
- Have a system for gaining your children's attention that is appropriate for their age. Reception children may enjoy '1, 2, 3 look at me ...' while Year 6 may respond better to a 'hands up' routine. Teachers use a variety of methods to gain children's attention, such as countdown systems, a bell or a musical instrument, or a catch-phrase or piece of music. Whichever method you use, do so in a consistent manner and make sure that you have sanctions planned for the occasions when children fail to comply

with your expectations. It is perfectly acceptable to change systems after a period of time, especially for young children as they tend to become bored with a particular method.

- It is worth finding some way of recording rewards given out, especially as house or team points. There is a lot of evidence to suggest that it is either the more able children or the challenging children who receive most rewards. The 'average' children who just get on and do their best often go unrecognized and unrewarded.
- Where possible, share your lesson plan with teaching assistants who will be working with you in your lessons. Make sure that your expectations, rules, rewards and sanctions have been made absolutely transparent to these colleagues, and make sure that you fully empower them to support you in your drive towards good behaviour. Make it clear what you want them to do when they spot children misbehaving.
- Ensure that all of your resources have been fully prepared, are easily accessible and you have planned how they will be distributed during your lesson. The smooth distribution of resources is one way of avoiding those 'break in flow' points that disrupt lessons and which offer children full opportunities to become distracted. You may decide to have children working as monitors to distribute resources or you may involve your TA. For some lessons, particularly practical ones, you may want to have all resources laid out on the tables ready for the lesson. In these situations, you may have to warn children not to handle them before they are directed to do so. For example, at the end of the morning session you may wish to say 'this afternoon when you come back after lunch, there will be lots of resources for art laid out on the table – it's important you don't touch these, but come and sit on the carpet straightaway.'
- Make sure that you include as many elements of your behaviour management in your lesson plans as possible. For example, you might write 'remind children about rules for working in groups' or 'set expectations about noise levels'. As you get more experienced, you will not need to do this to the same extent.

Interactive and relationship issues (Personal and Clinical Domains)

- Make sure that you learn names as quickly as possibly. Using a name establishes a psychological contract between you both, and makes it harder for the children to misbehave.
- Talk to your mentor and find out about the social and academic background of the children, so that you can begin to understand why the

children behave as they do. It is important to find out what works best for specific children.

- Always speak respectfully to the children even if you have to tell them off and issue a sanction. Make it clear that it is their behaviour that you are unhappy about and that you bear them no grudge as individuals.

- Try to catch them doing things well. Take every opportunity to praise them directly or, if you need to use a more subtle and indirect approach, make effective use of 'proximity praise'. This simply involves praising the behaviour of those children in direct proximity to the miscreant, in an attempt to influence his or her behaviour in a positive manner. The issue of proximity praise is explored in more detail in Chapter 10 of *Managing Your Classroom* (Dixie, 2007).

- Hard as it may be, you are advised not to lose your temper. The message is simple here: if you lose control of yourself you will lose control of the class. Having said this, there will be occasions when you will need to raise your voice in order to gain the full attention of the class. Having done this, lower the pitch of your voice while still using an assertive and firm tone.

- Whatever you do, do not talk over children's noise. If you do this you will have established the fact that it is acceptable for them to talk while you are talking. It is important for you to wait until the class is silent before you move on. Ensure that you support this with a firm sanction; otherwise you will simply have to repeat this performance every time you want to get your children's attention.

- Spend time talking with some of the more challenging children and finding out what makes them tick. It is amazing what you can find out when you really try. Both authors have experience of doing this and of seeing it done by other teachers. A good example is a headteacher who used football as a way of working with some of his more challenging boys. He would stop them around school and comment on how their team had performed at the weekend. This afforded them status and self-esteem, and established a climate of mutual respect. They were certainly more prepared to behave for him as he had shown an interest in them.

- It is human nature to want to be liked, and it is true that if you are liked by the children, you are more likely to be able to motivate and encourage them. However, being liked should be a by-product of being a good teacher, and not an aim. Some trainees are very reluctant to issue sanctions as they fear children will not like them as a result. Actually the opposite is true. All children want teachers to be fair and to ensure the rules are followed. They respect teachers who have good discipline.

- If children are off-task try to use positive phraseology. Instead of saying something like, 'Stop messing about', you need to adopt a more positive stance by presuming the best of them. You could then say something like, 'Do you need some help with this, Gary?'

- Do not overreact if any of your children refuse to carry out your instructions or tell you that they are not going to do the work. Simply smile, adopt a positive tone and ask again. If this does not work, you will have to talk to your mentor about an appropriate way forward.
- Where individuals are displaying challenging behaviour, you need to offer them 'choice direction'. Choice direction simply means giving them alternative scenarios. For example, if a child is playing with a toy car you could say something like, 'You can either give the car to me and collect it at the end of the day, or you can put it into your bag.' Given the 'closed' nature of these directions, most children will choose the latter option
- Lastly, don't be afraid to ask for help from your mentor.

When we work with primary trainees on aspects of behaviour management, we introduce them to the 'Golden Rules'. These are listed on the audit sheet below, along with a grading system. We ask trainees to grade themselves on each one, and for their mentors to do this independently. Then they compare their grades. This can then be used to help trainees move forward in each aspect. By concentrating on one rule at a time, the trainees gradually improve their technique.

Behaviour management audit	1	2	3	4	5
Has 'presence' in the classroom					
Never accepts an answer which is called out					
Never speaks while the children are speaking					
Gains attention very quickly at start					
Uses lots of praise					
Uses sanctions when necessary					
Effective strategies for gaining attention					
Able to hold children's attention while talking mid-lesson					
Has effective methods for tidying away					
Has developed 'the look'					
Uses voice well to manage behaviour					
Has high expectations, for example says things like 'I expect you to…'					
Gets the same level of behaviour if mentor absent					
Able to use same strategies in practical subjects, for example PE					

25 Lesson-planning

All good teaching requires careful planning. As you can see from Table 25.1, planning can occur on three or four levels. Most schools will have similar types of plans for each year group in each subject.

Table 25.1 Sample plans

Long-term plans	The yearly plan includes a description of the topics required to be covered and the expected teaching order.
Medium-term plans	This plan is usually produced on a termly or half-termly basis, and could range from a simple framework to a very prescriptive set of plans.
Weekly plans	Some schools use these as their lesson-planning documents, particularly literacy and numeracy from the primary frameworks.
Lesson plans	The day-to-day planning of individual lessons.

All training providers require their trainees to prepare, and work from, a formal lesson plan for **every** lesson (or part-lesson) taught. As outlined in Table 25.1, the lesson plan should evolve from the medium-term or weekly plan. Although you will initially be required to work on the lesson plan with the close support of your mentor, you will soon be able to produce these on your own. Having said this, you will probably still need to get them checked over by your mentor before you teach your lesson.

The point of a lesson plan is to guide you in organizing yourself, your resources and your additional adult support with the purpose of helping your children to achieve the intended learning outcomes. It requires you to think about exactly what you want the children to learn, and then to think through the sequence of activities which will enable the children to achieve this. Some courses require you to use their specific layout for planning, while others let you use your own format. An example of a lesson plan is shown in Figure 25.1 on p. 175, but there is no one single format for successful lesson-planning. Having said this, you do need to be aware that there are a number of key elements that make for good planning. Although you will be required to present your lesson plan to your mentor and your tutor, you do need to remember that the main audience for the lesson plan is **you**. Before you start planning your lessons you might like to consider the following prompt questions.

1. What is the purpose of the lesson?
2. What are the objectives for the lesson?
3. What is the best way for these children to achieve these?
4. What differentiated activities or tasks will help them to achieve?
5. What is the minimum amount of time needed for each task or activity?
6. What will happen when different children take different amounts of time to do a task?
7. What extension activities can I provide for those children who finish their work early?
8. How much time do I set aside to settle the class, take the register, introduce the topic, hand out equipment or books, clear up and dismiss the children?
9. What materials and resources will I need to assemble before the lesson?
10. Have I catered for my EAL, SEN and/or G and T children?
11. How will my TA support learning?
12. How will I assess the children's learning?

In Key Stage 1 and 2, some lessons will have three distinct sections, namely an introduction, differentiated activities and a plenary. However, there are many variations to this structure and it really depends on what you are teaching. Sometimes the lesson will begin with an activity and there will be more direct teaching in the middle of the lesson. However, a traditionally structured lesson will look roughly as follows:

Introduction

The introductory phase of the lesson requires you to tell the children the objective. In some schools this is introduced by the character WALT (We are learning to ...) and WILF (What I am looking for ...) as suggested by Clarke (2001). It is also the part of the lesson that requires you to consolidate and review the learning that has occurred in previous lessons and then make links with new learning scenarios. This phase of the lesson requires you to **introduce** new concepts and content to the children and put these into a context, using language they are likely to understand. This is also a good time and place to model examples of good practice as a means of raising children's expectations of their performances. It will involve visual, auditory and kinaesthetic learners. The visual element is achieved through using resources such as the interactive whiteboard, puppets, subject-specific equipment or video clips; the auditory by teacher and children's discussion, and the kinaesthetic by using mini-whiteboards, number-lines, child participation on the whiteboard or role-play. The teacher will use this time to explain what the children will be doing in the next part of the lesson. If explaining different activities to different groups, this becomes a challenge in itself!

Main body

The main phase of the lesson requires you to provide children with an in-depth exploration of these new concepts and skills. This is the part of the lesson when you would expect children to complete their tasks and activities, in groups, pairs or on an individual basis. The main body of the lesson should contain a range of activities and should offer opportunities for children of different abilities and learning styles to achieve. You and your TA may be working with different groups, but at the same time this is also the phase of the lesson where you need to monitor all the children's learning. You need to make opportunities to assess their understanding of and ability to complete the tasks you have set, as well as giving them feedback and guidance.

Plenary

The concluding phase of the lesson requires you to consolidate and assess the learning that has just taken place. This could be done through a question/answer session; sharing of work; talk partners; class discussion; quizzes/games. Your job as a teacher is to reframe the responses given to you by the children, and then to summarize the learning that has occurred during the lesson. Although good teachers will constantly monitor and assess children's learning as they teach, rather than simply waiting until the end of the lesson, most of you will not yet have the skills to do this. This makes your plenary session even more important. Your plenary session needs to be designed to assess the degree to which your learning objectives have been realized. The final part of the lesson should see you linking the learning that has just occurred to the content of the next lesson.

In reception and nursery classrooms, the way of working will be very different. There will be fewer times when you are teaching the whole class together and more times when children will be choosing what they do. You will be planning for adult-directed activities and organizing opportunities for children to learn through playing with a selection of resources. There will also be a need to plan activities and resources for learning outside. For example, you may talk to the whole class about a letter which has been sent to the class by a cuddly toy. This may introduce new vocabulary and the terminology associated with posting letters. After this there may be opportunities for the children to play in the role-play post office, to write letters of their own or to design stamps. There may also be other activities planned which are connected to the theme or season, as well as a range of other equipment children may choose to play with. Increasingly these types of activity are being incorporated into Year 1 and even Year 2 classes. Some of these classrooms have 'learning tables' where the teacher works with a group, while the other children choose activities inside and outdoors.

What needs to be in your lesson plan?

Contextual information

This part of the plan should give information which provides a background to the lesson and which sets the boundaries or limits of the plan, such as:

- the name of the subject and topic being studied
- the date and time of the lesson
- details of any SEN, EAL, and/or G and T children
- details of any children with social or behavioural problems
- a description of how this lesson fits into the learning sequence: i.e. what was learned previously and how this new learning will feed into future lessons.

Learning objectives

All lessons need **learning objectives.** You need to make it absolutely transparent what you expect the children to know, understand or be able to do by the end of the lesson. It is very common to confuse the tasks/activities that will be done in the lesson with learning objectives, so be very wary of doing this. Schools will use different systems for setting objectives, but it is expected that children will know – by being told or by seeing these displayed on the board – what the learning objectives are. When setting your learning objectives you could consider the following questions. By the end of this lesson, what should the children know? What should the children be able to understand? What should children be able to do? You should be able to assess whether children have achieved them or not. Some examples of clear learning objectives are:

- To be able to measure accurately using cms and mms.
- To be able to use interesting adjectives in a description of a setting.
- To understand why the Saxons invaded Britain.

Be wary of writing learning objectives that start:

- To learn about . . . (this is very vague. How will you know when children have learned it?).
- To explore . . . or to be aware of . . . (these are very hard to assess).
- To make . . . (this is an activity, not something they will learn. Think about what you want them to learn through doing that making activity).

If you are planning a lesson of a cross-curricular nature, make sure your learning objectives relate very specifically to one subject area. If you do not do this, your lesson will lose its focus, and your children may not make as much progress as they could. It is good practice to link areas together, but this must be done well. For example, you may choose to use the topic of Ancient Egypt to teach the children how to write in a persuasive manner. For example, the activity might be to write a letter persuading a museum curator who the best pharaoh was. You should keep your learning objectives literacy-focused in this scenario. Hopefully the children will be highly motivated as they can use their knowledge of this time period as a context for their writing.

Success criteria

You will need to think about and record some differentiated success criteria. That is, at the end of the lesson, how will you know that the least able (LA), medium ability (MA) and higher ability (HA) in the class have met the learning objective? What will they have achieved? For example:

LA: Will have used five adjectives in their descriptive writing which was guided by the TA.
MA: Will have chosen appropriate adjectives from a word-bank in their description.
HA: Will have used adventurous, original adjectives from dictionaries or other texts in their description.

If your success criteria are clear and well thought-out, it will make it easy for you to assess what the different groups have achieved, and so you will be able to evaluate your teaching and the children's learning.

Introduction

In this part of the plan, you will have to describe what you are going to do, and what you will use to do it. Make sure that you have listed key vocabulary to be introduced and key questions you need to ask. This is vital if you want to ensure you move the children's learning on. You need to ask yourself what vocabulary they need to learn in this lesson. You should include details of what you want the TA to do in this part of the lesson. You may have a specific starter activity which you need to plan here. For example, most numeracy lessons begin with a mental and oral starter which may or may not be connected to the main part of the lesson.

Main activities

When selecting the activities and tasks you intend to use in your lesson, you need to think about the following key questions:

- Will the tasks and activities enable the learning objective(s) to be met?
- How are the tasks and activities going to enthuse and engage children of all ability levels?
- How successful will your tasks and activities be in catering for the different types of learners in your lesson?
- How can you use these tasks and activities to assess learning?

You need to decide which group you and the TA will be mainly working with.

Plenary

Many trainees find that, because of their lack of experience in planning effectively, this phase of the lesson often gets squeezed out. However, you do need to know that this is a crucial part of the lesson because, if it is carried out properly, it will provide you and the children with an indication as to whether the learning objectives have been met. There is a range of different formats for the plenary. The suggestions below only scratch the surface and you need to carry out more specific and focused research into this aspect of your teaching.

- Verbal or written quizzes supported by a follow-up discussion.
- Question-answer session in which you select children from a range of abilities to respond.
- Providing children with new scenarios in which to apply their newly gained knowledge, understanding and/or skills.
- Asking children to refer back to the learning objectives and provide evidence from the lesson to show how these have been met.

- Drama activities such as hot-seating to demonstrate and recall information.
- Paired work where children share what they have learned or still do not understand.

Assessment opportunities

This is the section where you have to write how you will find out whether the children have learned what you want them to learn. That is, how do you know they have achieved the success criteria you have set? You will have to think carefully about how you can assess this at each stage of the lesson. For example, in the introduction you may want to include questions you will ask to determine understanding. In the main part of the lesson you may observe a particular group and ask a TA to complete an assessment proforma. In the plenary you should plan to discover what learning has taken place, as well as any misconceptions and concerns which you can address next lesson.

Evaluation and reflection

To a greater or lesser degree, all trainees are expected to evaluate their lessons and reflect upon ways in which to improve their practice. You may find that your training provider has furnished you with a set of questions to be answered or a set of instructions to be followed. Alternatively, they may leave you entirely to your own devices to do this. If the latter situation is the case, you could use the reflective formula provided in Chapter 13. Whichever method you use to evaluate and reflect upon your performances and on the quality of learning in the lesson, you do need to identify **and act** upon the specific targets identified for your development.

Trainee:	**Subject**	Year group:
Date:	Time:	TA:

Learning objective:

Success criteria:

LA:

MA:

HA:

National Curriculum/Framework links:

Use of additional adults: (more detail on additional support sheet)

Context:

Resources (including ICT):

Introduction:

Key vocabulary and questions:

Main part of lesson:

Activities:

Plenary:

Assessment opportunities:

Evaluation of teaching:

Evaluation of learning:

Target for the future:

Figure 25.1 Exemplar lesson plan

Resources

Try to be as creative as possible when resourcing your lessons. There are numerous ways you can engage children and help them to achieve the learning objectives. There are obviously specific subject resources available in schools, but there are also many things you can use which you can find at home or online. Some suggestions are included below.

Interactive whiteboard

There are endless resources available online – it is just a question of researching them! A few useful websites are listed below:

www.sparklebox.co.uk
www.scholastic.co.uk
http://kids.nationalgeographic.com/kids
www.bbc.co.uk/learning/
www.primaryresources.co.uk

Toys/games etc

Puppets are a wonderful resource for introducing topics; discussing personal and social issues; behaviour management; friendship issues, and so on.

Toys – construction bricks, small world play, model cars, construction kits, dolls, jigsaws, board-games and play-dough – are good for all aspects of the primary curriculum.

Props/dressing-up clothes etc

It is amazing what you can find at home in terms of hats, gloves, scarves, masks, pieces of fabric, sunglasses, ribbon and so on, that you can use for drama and creative writing. It is incredible how a shawl can transform a child into a different character and give her the confidence to use his or her imagination to enter a different world.

Junk materials

When you enter the world of primary teaching, you start to envisage a thousand uses for a cardboard roll, shoe-box or yoghurt pot! Start building up a collection for use in maths (capacity), technology (models), literacy (story-boxes) and science (experiments).

Books

Start to build up a collection of children's fiction – especially picture-books. These don't have to be new – scour second-hand bookshops, school fairs, jumble sales and charity shops. Stories are a great way to introduce concepts, convey messages and build relationships.

Kits/bags/boxes

Teachers collect wonderful resources which can be used for imaginative work such as story-writing. We have come across the following recently:

- Story-boxes – shoe-boxes set up to contain all the elements of a story such as Lego characters, props, fabric and so on, so children can use them to retell stories, make up their own endings etc.
- Story sacks – random or closely linked items in a drawstring bag which children use to develop story ideas.
- Curiosity kits – theme-based bags linked to topic work that enrich and extend children's learning.
- Treasure boxes – small boxes containing beautiful things such as marbles, jewels, glitter, and so on, to stimulate story-writing and story-telling.

26 Engaging your class

There is no doubt that keeping the children active and fully engaged in your lessons will have extremely positive knock-on effects in terms of behaviour management and learning. To this end, therefore, you need to do everything you can to keep your children focused, on-task and motivated. In order to help you to do this, guidance is offered on a number of relevant issues below.

Giving instructions to classes

Giving instructions to children is more difficult than it seems. Our observations of both teachers and trainees at work in the classroom have highlighted to us the importance of giving transparent instructions to children. Failure to do so can result in them losing interest and veering off-task. The importance of this is compounded if you are teaching practical lessons where children have a degree of freedom to use the resources located at various points in the classroom. When determining the specific instructions you want your children to follow, use these guidelines which have been taken from *Managing Your Classroom* (Dixie, 2007).

- **Keep it simple and choose instructions that are observable.**

Choose a limited number of instructions for each classroom activity. Try to give them all the instructions before they start. Whenever possible, model exactly what you want the children to do. Reinforce the instructions by having a written or pictorial list for them to follow, and remind them of this in the lesson.

- **Tell them *how* you want them to do the activity, as well as what you want them to do.**

Use adverbs so they know what your expectations are: 'I want you to cut out the shapes *carefully*.' Include instructions about how you want them to behave and, if necessary, how you want them to work together.

- **Involve the class.**

Ask questions while you are explaining and at the end of the instructions such as 'What is the first thing you have to do?' When you have finished explaining what the children have to do, say 'Put your hands up if you are uncertain about what to do'. This is a better question than 'Does everyone know what to do?' which is an open invitation to everyone to call out 'yes'.

Using an effective questioning technique

Much research has been carried out to show that good questioning techniques lie at the heart of effective learning. In the early stages of your career you are advised to produce a list of questions in your lesson plan. It is really important to involve as many children as possible in your question-answer and discussion sessions. By doing so, you will provide them with a high degree of ownership of the lesson, and you will soon note significant and positive effects of this.

Points to consider are:

- **Try different techniques for managing questions.**

You might want to start with the 'hands-up rule' which many teachers use. This has the advantage of enabling you to see who either knows the answer or is confident to 'have a go'. However, it precludes many children, some of whom may 'switch off', knowing you will not ask them, and some who are simply not confident enough to volunteer an answer. When you get to know the children better, try the method where you ask specific questions to individuals by name. This means you keep all the children on their toes, knowing they may be asked. It is essential to know which children you can ask in this scenario, otherwise children may feel intimidated and/or even very uncomfortable. Whichever method or combination of methods you use, you need to make it clear to the children, otherwise they will be confused. Take this example of a Year 2 boy: 'I don't know whether to put my hand up or not. If I do, she asks someone who hasn't got their hand up. Then if I don't put my hand up, she asks someone who has.'

- **Try to ask more 'open' than 'closed' questions.**

These will make children really think, rather than search for the answer they think you want. Many trainees seek answers to questions which are a bit like 'think of the word that is in my head'. If you find yourself saying 'It begins with S . . .' just tell them what the word is! Questions should make children think – it is not a guessing-game!

- **Decide when questions are important for the learning.**

We often see time wasted at the beginning of lessons when trainees could simply remind children of what they did last lesson, rather than trying to get them to remember what they did. Many of the children will find this really hard – just tell them!

- **Create a positive environment for questions.**

This is essential if you want children to answer freely and confidently and ask questions. You have to find ways of valuing all contributions and making children feel good about joining in, even if they get the answer wrong. Comments such as 'Well tried Joe, that's a good try' or 'That's not the right answer Chloe, but I'm really glad you had a go' will make them want to have another go. However, be wary of praising or accepting wrong answers. For example, if you ask the children for the term that means 'see through' in science, you might get the response 'flexible'. It would not help to say 'almost right, well tried'. You will then have left the children thinking that the word 'flexible' is very like the word 'transparent'. You also have to make sure that children know how to respond to their peers' wrong answers. They have to be taught to value everyone's contribution, and not to laugh or snigger when their peers get things wrong.

- **Differentiate your questions.**

As you become more experienced you will be able to do this with ease. In whole-class sessions you will be able to ask the able children more challenging questions and will simplify questions for some of the least able. In this way, a lot of them may not even realize this is happening and, even if they do, they will all appreciate it. Make sure you praise the contributions of less-confident children, as they need to be encouraged to participate. All children need opportunities to verbalize their learning. They also need to develop confidence to speak in front of larger audiences. This is a skill which they will need throughout their education and into later life.

- **Be aware of whom you are asking.**

Make sure that you do not ask a disproportionate number of questions to any particular group of children. For example, are you asking as many boys as girls? Are you addressing more questions to the most able children?

Using ICT to support your professional practice

27

There is no doubt that the use of ICT helps to increase children's motivation, confidence and self-esteem levels. Effective use of ICT enhances their social and cooperative skills, and helps to improve overall academic achievement. ICT is deemed to be such an important ingredient in the teacher trainee's repertoire, that it has three QTS standards, partially or wholly dedicated to this aspect of your pedagogic practice. These are:

> Q16 Have passed the professional skills test in numeracy, literacy and information and communication technology.
>
> Q17 Know how to use skills in literacy, numeracy and ICT to support their teaching and wider professional activities.
>
> Q23 Design opportunities for learners to develop their literacy, numeracy and ICT skills.

The drive towards an increased use of ICT has been initiated by the TDA which has funded e-learning projects for teacher-training providers on a national basis. In the words of the TDA:

> We share the view expressed by the ITT community that the ability to work experimentally helps to create a culture of innovation and change which is central to developing activity and quality in initial teacher training.
>
> (www.tda.gov.uk/partners/quality/ict/supportforictinitt.aspx)

In 2006–7, in an effort to introduce innovation, the TDA targeted the following eight areas:

- video conferencing
- video capture and analysis
- PDAs
- laptops for trainees/tablet PCs for trainers
- innovative work in ICT

- interactive whiteboards
- subject-specific software
- ICT-driven subject-specific hardware, for example CAD-CAM and data-loggers.

The TDA's big push towards using innovative ICT techniques in the classroom has led to training providers being required to audit and monitor the ICT skills of their trainees. So how exactly does this affect you? In the initial stages of your training, you will be asked to complete an audit of your ICT skills and of your knowledge and understanding of the role of ICT in the classroom. Having completed your audit, you will need to identify specific 'areas for development' to work on. You will be expected to be competent in using ICT in your professional role, so that you are able to operate the ICT systems used in different schools and adapt to change and innovation. In the early stages of your training, you are expected to be competent in the programs/skills presented to you in the following list.

Word-processing For example using tables, inserting pictures and graphs, creating page layouts, adding text boxes and speech bubbles, adding page numbers, adjusting margins and layouts, using the drawing toolbar, using headers and footers.

Spreadsheets Creating a spreadsheet, using a spreadsheet as a database, drawing graphs, making calculations per cell, using pre-defined functions such as MIN, MAX, AVERAGE, sorting data, organizing data on multiple worksheets.

PowerPoint Making presentation slides, adding images to slides, adding videos and sound files to slides, changing fonts and background colours, inserting hyperlinks, running slide-show in classroom, printing handouts.

Desktop publishing Showing some familiarity with what these packages can do. Investigate the use of desktop publishing software such as Microsoft Publisher to create classroom displays and banners.

Use of the internet Being able to use a web-browser effectively (typing web address in address bar, amending the address book). Being able to use search engines effectively to search for web pages or for pictures, downloading material from the internet or from an attachment retrieving information in different format (text, picture, video) from the internet to reuse in a different piece of software, and so on).

Email Being able to send and receive emails, reply to and forward emails, send files as attachments, send hyperlinked web pages, save and sort emails into sub-folders.

IWB technology Being confident in using interactive whiteboard effectively and efficiently.

> **Saving documents** Saving to school network/intranet; to CD; saving to USB portable drive, memory stick. Being able to transfer files from one computer to another (i.e. using a USB key), being able to take a backup of existing files, being able to organize files in folders and subfolders and rename/delete/move/duplicate files and folders.
>
> **Admin** Using school reporting system, accessing children's data from school system.
>
> **VLE/intranet** Showing some familiarity with how virtual learning environment can be used within a school. Show a willingness to see how the school you are working in uses a VLE or intranet.

You are also recommended to read your school's ICT policy document carefully and to become intimate with expected protocol. Your ICT policy document should make some firm recommendations as to how to make appropriate use of ICT in the classroom as well as in other areas of your professional career.

You need to be aware that your training providers will need you to provide evidence to show how you have continued to develop your application of ICT in the classroom and in other aspects of your professional practice. Although the exact format of these audits will differ according to each specific training provider, it is apposite to present you with an exemplar version in Figure 27.1.

Many ITT providers are now expecting schools to video their trainees at work. This is a hugely beneficial tool in your development. As a trainee, you should value this experience and use it as much as you can. It is a great privilege to be able to sit down with your mentor and analyse part of your lesson together. It is the only way you can really see what the children experience when you are teaching. You will notice your voice, mannerisms, body language and teacher presence, as well as being able to determine how clear your instructions and teaching points are. It is also interesting to watch individual children and the way they respond to you, which you may not notice when you are 'out front' monitoring the whole class.

Another useful device is the voice recorder. These are simple hand-held devices that basically record sound only – either your voice or your children's voices. Both can be valuable to you. This enables you to analyse your questioning techniques or to examine the feedback you give to children. Voice recorders can also be left with a group with whom you are not working closely to analyse their learning after the lesson. With a bit of imagination, you will find many uses for them!

First name		Surname	
Specialism		ITT course	

Do you have access to a computer at home? (tick your answer)			
No		Yes, but without internet access	
Yes, with dial-up internet access		Yes, with broadband internet access	

Use this key for the following questions:

3 = I can do this with confidence and could teach someone else how to do it.

2 = I know what this is, but I would need a hint or a reminder to show me how to do it.

1 = I do not know what this is and/or I will not be able to do it without being shown step by step.

Please try to be as truthful with your answers as possible. If you are uncertain which answer to select, choose the lower number.

Managing information (My Documents)			
Create a new folder in My Documents	3	2	1
Rename a folder	3	2	1
Copy files and paste them into a different folder	3	2	1
Select all the files in a folder	3	2	1
Transfer files to a pen drive	3	2	1
Tidy up your folders, then burn a backup CD of all your work	3	2	1

Gathering information on the internet (i.e. Internet Explorer)			
Use a search engine to find information on a specific issue	3	2	1
Use an image search to find a specific picture	3	2	1
Use an advanced search to narrow down the number of search results	3	2	1
Add a website to your internet favourites list	3	2	1
Create your own webpage and upload it onto the internet	3	2	1
Subscribe to a site using a RSS feed for updates	3	2	1
Create an online survey	3	2	1
Send and receive emails, insert file attachments and update a contact list	3	2	1

Have a live text chat with another person using MSN or equivalent	3	2	1
Download a podcast	3	2	1
Use a webcam to talk to another person	3	2	1
Research useful information	3	2	1

Analysing and processing information (i.e. Microsoft Excel)			
Input mark-book data into a spreadsheet model	3	2	1
Sort the data alphabetically by surname	3	2	1
Use auto sum to add up the data in one column	3	2	1
Use a formula to multiply two cells together	3	2	1
Use a formula to find the mean (average) of one column of data	3	2	1
Use a formula to find out the highest value in one column of data	3	2	1
Use the fill handle to transfer a formula into other cells	3	2	1
Create charts (bar, pie, line, etc.) and know which one to use when	3	2	1
Import a .csv file of data into a spreadsheet	3	2	1
Analyse survey data on recycling and create charts to show results	3	2	1

Word-processing information (i.e. Microsoft Word)			
Touch type	3	2	1
Format text to resize, change font, make bold	3	2	1
Use the align centre and align right buttons	3	2	1
Insert a clipart image and resize	3	2	1
Wordwrap text around an image	3	2	1
Crop an image	3	2	1
Insert the draw toolbar	3	2	1
Insert a table	3	2	1
Merge two cells in a table	3	2	1
Create a formal letter to a headteacher re a job application	3	2	1

Presenting information (i.e. Microsoft PowerPoint)			
Format the background using Fill Effects	3	2	1

Insert an AutoShape callout	3	2	1
Create a WordArt title	3	2	1
Animate an object on the slide	3	2	1
Insert images found from a website	3	2	1
Insert action buttons to link pages	3	2	1
Insert a hyperlink to website	3	2	1
Deliver a PowerPoint presentation to a group of people	3	2	1

Digital media (i.e. Microsoft Movie Maker and PhotoShop Elements)			
Use a digital stills camera and upload the images to a computer	3	2	1
Use a digital video camera and upload the footage to a computer	3	2	1
Use a microphone to record a narration as an audio file on the computer	3	2	1
Enhance a digital image by changing contrast, colour saturation, etc.	3	2	1
Compress an image to make it a smaller file size	3	2	1
Edit video footage and create a finished video	3	2	1

What other ICT skills do you have that were not mentioned in the survey?

What other ICT skills would you like to learn that were not mentioned in the survey?

Figure 27.1 ICT audit (reproduced by kind permission of Alex Savage, Notre Dame High School, Norwich)

Understanding the issue of inclusion

28

To engage all your children in the learning process, then you need to be aware of what is meant by the term 'inclusion'. This is a term that you will come across on a regular basis during your training and beyond. According to the Centre of Studies in Inclusive Education website (http://inclusion.uwe.ac.uk/csie/csiefaqs.htm) inclusion in education involves:

- valuing all children and staff equally
- increasing the participation of children in, and reducing their exclusion from, the cultures, curricula and communities of local schools
- restructuring the cultures, policies and practices in schools so that they respond to the diversity of children in the locality
- reducing barriers to learning and participation for all children, not just those with impairments or those who are categorized as 'having special educational needs'
- learning from attempts to overcome barriers to the access and participation of particular individuals to make changes for the benefit of children more widely
- viewing the differences between children as resources to support learning, rather than as problems to be overcome
- acknowledging the right of children to an education in their locality
- improving schools for staff as well as for children
- emphasizing the role of schools in building community and developing values, as well as in increasing achievement
- fostering mutually sustaining relationships between schools and communities.

What this actually means in practice is that all children and young people, regardless of gender, background, ability or culture, should now be able to learn together in all educational establishments and be provided with appropriate networks of support. Inclusion means enabling all children to participate in the life and work of mainstream institutions to the best of their abilities, whatever their needs. QTS standard Q19 states:

> Know how to make effective personalized provision for those they teach, including those for whom English is an additional language or who have special educational needs or disabilities, and how to take practical account of diversity and promote equality and inclusion in their teaching.

This means that you will have to ensure that all children in your class learn. You will be taught either by your provider or by the mentors you are working with what this entails. It means you will have to:

- differentiate your teaching so that children of all abilities learn, from those with special educational needs (SEN) to those who are gifted and talented (G and T).
- ensure you cater for the needs of boys and girls
- learn how to teach children with English as an additional language (EAL).

As previously said, it is impossible and indeed undesirable for all children to be taught on a one-to-one personal basis according to their needs. Most teachers consider three ability groups in their classes when they are planning, often known as the lower-ability children (LAPs), medium-ability children (MAPs) and higher-ability children (HAPs). Generally it would be expected that you differentiate questions to these groups when you are working with the whole class, and then plan for their needs and abilities when setting tasks and activities during the main part of the lesson. For example, you may decide to set slightly different activities, plan different resources for each group, plan for adult support for one group or expect a greater degree of independence from some. It is often not enough to differentiate 'by outcome' or by the quantity of work you expect them to produce. You may, however, set specific targets for each group for a particular activity which all children undertake. The targets may be, for example, about using adventurous vocabulary, full stops and capital letters, or good use of connectives.

However, trainees often find it most difficult to cater for those children at both extreme ends of the ability range as well as children who have English as an additional language, so we will now spend some time discussing those areas.

Working with SEN children

It is absolutely crucial that you keep up to date with the changes that regularly occur to the SEN Code of Practice. You can find a copy of this document at the following web address: www.teachernet.gov.uk/docbank/index.cfm?id=3724

The school is highly likely to have used this document to inform its own special SEN policy, but there will be individual nuances with which you need to make yourself familiar. You also need to be extremely proactive at the beginning of each of your school practices in making sure that you meet with the special needs coordinator (SENCO) to discuss the characteristics of each of your SEN children. You also need to seek the advice of the SENCO as to the best ways to simplify the work for these children. Bearing in mind the vast array of special educational needs, it is not possible in this book to offer specific strategies to cater for each of the conditions. However, a list of generalized guidance that may help to support the learning and inclusion of the SEN children in your classes is set out below. You can make use of these strategies until such time as you can seek advice on how to deal with the specific SEN cases in your lessons.

Some top tips for teaching SEN children

- Make sure that you have read their individual education plans (IEPs).
- Set differentiated learning objectives to allow these children to succeed
- Make sure that you provide a strong context for the learning. More than most, they need to see the relevance of the learning.
- Provide these children with a lot of one-to-one contact, either with you or with your teaching assistant(s). However, it is important that they can work independently too, otherwise they become dependent on an adult.
- Provide non-threatening but, nevertheless, challenging tasks and activities.
- Provide them with short structured tasks.
- Provide clear written instructions in bullet-point fashion.
- Make sure that you demonstrate or model your learning outcomes. SEN children need to know exactly what they are expected to do.
- Ensure frequent repetition of keywords, subject content or concepts.
- If possible, support your text with visual images such as pictures or video clips.
- Make full use of interactive ICT as this helps them to redraft their work and produce work that looks presentable.
- Provide a range of opportunities for these children to demonstrate what they know and what they can do. This could be through the media of: drama, artwork, poetry, storyboards, cartoons, flow diagrams, bullet-point lists, diagrams, puzzles, true/false quizzes, games, and so on.
- Make sure that the assessment reflects the children's learning and does not discriminate by structure or language.
- Promote high self-esteem by overtly valuing everyone's contribution.

Working with gifted and talented children

According to the DCSF, gifted and talented learners are defined as those who have one or more abilities developed to a level significantly ahead of their year group (or with the potential to develop those abilities).

Gifted describes learners who have the ability to excel academically in one or more subjects such as English, drama or technology.

Talented describes learners who have the ability to excel in practical skills such as sport, leadership or artistic performance, or in an applied skill.

All schools are encouraged to identify the children in each year group who fit these definitions. The DCSF publication *Identifying Gifted and Talented Learners – Getting Started* provides more detail on this process, providing information for teachers leading this initiative in schools. As a trainee, you need to be aware of these children and to try to provide learning activities in the classroom which offer additional challenge through a combination of acceleration, enrichment and extension. Some ideas you could try would be to:

- ask more open-ended questions that require a higher level of thinking
- plan activities at the upper end of Bloom's Taxonomy that require children to analyse, apply and evaluate rather than just recall and remember
- set up opportunities for more independent research
- widen the scope of a topic – for example, further aspects of Tudor life, using larger numbers in problem-solving, comparing a poem studied in class with others by the same author
- ask children to summarize information in a small number of words – a difficult skill!
- ask them to make up their own questions for research or problems to solve in maths
- get them to research 'another time, another place', which is good for history and geography. For example, what was happening in England when Ancient Egypt had pharaohs?

Try not to get them doing **more** of something, helping someone else do their work, colouring-in or just reading a book. None of these have the element of challenge these children need.

Working with children for whom English is an additional language

In the true spirit of inclusive education, you need to provide appropriate learning opportunities for those children for whom the English language is not their mother-tongue. It is therefore absolutely vital that you familiarize yourself with your school's EAL policy and that you use this newly acquired knowledge and understanding to inform your lesson-planning.

Speak to your mentor and discuss the level descriptors for English provided for you in Appendix 2. In the early stages of your practice, try to involve your mentor in the planning of opportunities for these children in your lessons. Do not be frightened to ask whether they have any ideas or resources you can use. It is important that when you come to record their current levels of achievement, you include an additional column in your mark-book for their specific levels of English. You need to use your regular meetings with your mentor to clarify any issues you are not certain about. Make sure that you record the general flavour of your conversation in your meetings logs as this will provide firm evidence for a QTS standard that many trainees find difficulty in realizing.

Just as all English-speaking children are different and have their own individual learning needs, so too with EAL children. It is crucial that you remember that their fluency in speaking, reading and writing English does not necessarily reflect their cognitive ability. Do not be seduced into the 'one size fits all' model of provision for them. Having said this, it is fair to say that there are certain generalized principles involved in the teaching of EAL children, and to this end a number of strategies are listed below:

- Make sure that you carry out some basic research into the cultural and personal backgrounds of the EAL children in your classes. If possible, include words from their first language in displays in your classroom.
- Give them lots of opportunities to engage in dialogue with other children.
- Identify any 'cultural content' that may be unfamiliar to them and be prepared to explain this, perhaps drawing parallels with other cultures.
- Ensure that you start each lesson by explaining the key vocabulary. Make sure you provide your EAL children with a visual version of the glossary of terms to put into their books.
- Make sure that you repeat and summarize instructions and requests, but be very careful not to vary your language too much when you repeat yourself. This may result in the child spending unnecessary time working out if there is a difference between the two messages. Moderate your speed of delivery to meet the needs of these children.
- Wherever possible, give practical demonstrations to these children. Supporting your words with actions is a highly effective way of conveying a message to them. However, you do need to be highly sensitive to the fact that body language and gestures vary in meaning between cultures.

In many cultures children are taught to avoid making eye contact with their elders.

- Do not over-correct their mistakes, as this will soon cause them to become demotivated. Have a specific focus when assessing their work and when setting targets.
- When providing work for these children, make sure that you differentiate. For example: single-word answers are acceptable from children who are new to English, but with increasing experience they must be encouraged to expand their answers and use full sentences.
- Encourage risk-taking within a safe and secure environment. Create a 'can do' culture within the classroom and have high expectations of them. Expect them to succeed.
- Where possible find opportunities to use role-play and drama.
- Make use of writing-frames, but only if children have had the opportunity to talk through their work prior to the written task.

Understanding assessment

29

This is probably one of the most important areas you will have to get to grips with in your training. In many ways, it should be the first chapter in this section, as it is vital in informing everything you do. However, it is included here, as it makes more sense as a concept once you have started to get your head around some of the other issues.

There are two major types of assessment – summative and formative. **Summative assessment** describes the way in which teachers find out how much children know at the end of a unit of work. It takes place after the teaching and learning. This may be carried out in the form of a test or an assessed piece of work against particular National Curriculum levels. It gives a quantitative set of data, such as a level, number of correct answers or a grade. **Formative assessment** is the process by which teachers find out what children know, understand and can do throughout lessons on a day-to-day basis, and uses this to inform their planning. It includes observation, questioning and marking, and gives lots of information about the mistakes children are making, their thinking processes and their confidence. This data is more qualitative by nature, and often harder to record.

In recent years there has been much emphasis placed on this formative process to raise achievement, and it has become known as 'assessment for learning' (AfL). This includes the above features of formative assessment, but is based on the idea that children will improve most if they understand the aim of their learning, where they are in relation to this aim and how they can achieve the aim. It involves the following principles:

- sharing learning objectives with pupils
- sharing success criteria for groups of children
- helping pupils know and recognize the standards to aim for
- providing feedback that helps pupils to identify how to improve
- believing that every pupil can improve in comparison with previous achievements

- both teacher and pupils reviewing and reflecting on pupils' performance and progress
- pupils learning self-assessment techniques to discover areas in which they need to improve
- recognizing that both motivation and self-esteem, crucial for effective learning and progress, can be increased by effective assessment techniques.

You need to be fully aware that 'assessment for learning' is a key issue in teaching today, and features heavily in the standards you will have to achieve as a trainee. It will provide a focus for many a lesson observation on your school practices. It is worth getting to grips with this topic and spending some time exploring the various strategies you could deploy in your lessons. Ultimately it will help you plan effectively for subsequent lessons.

One of the hardest parts of teaching practice is pitching the lesson at the right level, especially when you don't know the children very well. Assessment is the key to getting this right. It is vital to become familiar with the curriculum for the year group you are teaching, but it is also essential to talk to the children before you teach them anything. We ask trainees to try to spend five minutes with a mixed-ability group of children talking about an aspect they are due to teach the next week. They are effectively 'assessing' where their children are – what they know, understand and can do at the present time. They can then plan more effectively for all groups. If you don't know the children, it is very hard to plan a lesson! The plenary is obviously very important too. It is important to use it to find out what the children have learned and where to pitch your next lesson in the sequence.

All in all, assessment is a very complicated process, but unless you get to grips with it, you will find it difficult to plan appropriately for the children you are teaching.

On top of this, you have to find a way to record all the information you are finding out too, whether formative or summative. That is the time to learn from your mentor about manageable record-keeping systems, be they sticky notes, tick-sheets or photographs. Whichever methods you use, you will need to draw on your records effectively for parents' evenings, writing reports and for transfer documents for the next teachers at the end of the school year.

Ofsted inspections 30

The Office for Standards in Education (Ofsted) sends inspectors into schools to examine all aspects of school life. The inspection should focus on the quality of teaching and learning, but inspectors will also look at the effectiveness of school management and budgeting systems and issues such as health and safety and the quality of the school environment. At the heart of every Ofsted inspection should be the academic and social welfare of the children.

As trainees, you need to be fully aware of the stressful nature of an Ofsted inspection. Although you are highly unlikely to be personally involved in the process, you need to know that there will be implications for you during this period. The three days given to schools as notice of an inspection are usually spent in a frenetic manner by all the members of staff. The prime aims for the staff over these three days will be to get their paperwork up to date, to make the school look as attractive as possible and to produce imaginative and enjoyable lessons for the children. Whatever your views on the efficacy and/or morality of what you see going on around you, you do need to be aware that this is a very vulnerable time for all staff. Be prepared to receive less personal help prior to and during the inspection period. It is possible that your regular weekly meetings and observations will be cancelled by your mentor. Although there is not really much you can do about this, you are advised to let your tutor know about the situation. Try to remember that teaching is very much a team-game and make it your business to offer help to staff in your school in getting ready for the inspection. It is this willingness to collaborate with colleagues that can go a long way.

Hopefully the information, guidance and advice proffered to you within this section will help to support you in your teaching practices. Although it is fully understandable that in a competitive world, it is tempting to focus your efforts on gaining a good teaching practice grade, you need to take a much broader view of the process than this. We hope that you achieve the grades you feel to be commensurate with your worth, but it is more important for you to treat your teaching-practice experiences in the spirit in which they have been designed – as practice for a life in teaching.

Part Seven
LOOKING AHEAD TO YOUR INDUCTION YEAR

Your first appointment 31

Although many of the anxieties about starting at your practice schools will soon disappear as you become acclimatized to your new environment, it is likely that you will then start to worry about looking for a job for next year. Although this will be a time of great uncertainty, you do need to be careful that this anxiety and insecurity do not lead you to make rash decisions and accept a job that you will regret for some time. Lots of trainees face this dilemma – should they take the first job that is offered to them, or should they wait for something that is more their ideal first post? Sometimes it is a matter of economics – you may well need a job to repay loans or support a family, in which case it would be foolish to turn one down. You also have to remember that jobs are not for ever – it is important to get your induction year as an NQT out of the way, then you can be more selective when you apply for a second post.

In their drive to fill their teaching vacancies, some of you may be offered jobs by your practice schools. There are two things to remember here. First, do not feel tempted to accept a job simply because you feel flattered to be offered the position. If the job is not right for you, then once the novelty of having your ego massaged has worn off, you will soon regret making this decision. Second, do not accept a job in a practice school simply because you are used to, and are relatively comfortable with, the school systems. If the culture and ethos of the school fail to match your expectations then the message is simple – seek a post elsewhere. However, if you still have not acquired a post as the year draws towards its climax, you will probably not be able to adopt such a balanced approach towards the decision-making process.

You also need to be aware of the market forces that are prevalent even within the teaching profession. These changes in market forces can be caused by rising and falling birth-rates, TDA recruitment drives and/or the salary levels offered by the government of the day. At times, when there is a teacher surplus, even teacher trainees with top grades are often turned down whereas in times of teacher shortage, schools will unashamedly hunt down trainees.

Geographical location and type of school can also influence the availability of vacant teaching posts. There is no doubt that, although extremely rewarding, it is often far more difficult to teach in a school situated in a deprived inner-city area than it is in a middle-class rural area. The desirability of a teaching post may, therefore, be mirrored by the number of applications made to any particular school. You will have to consider which type of school appeals to you. Hopefully you will have had a range of experiences in your practices, and will be able to make well-thought-out decisions.

The decision as to where to apply for your first teaching post may be influenced by your personal, social, cultural and/or religious background. For some of you, your choice of area will be dramatically reduced because you will not want to leave friends and family. For others, however, geographical mobility will simply not be an issue. It is also fair to say that your own philosophy towards education can be an important factor when deciding where to apply for jobs. It is also about personal preference – from your experience, you will have to decide whether you prefer small, large, urban or rural.

So, why is making the right choice of school so important? After all, can't you simply move on at the end of the year? In order to address these questions, we need to furnish you with some vital information about your induction year. It is extremely important to find a supportive school because, if you do fail your induction year, you are not given a second chance to qualify as a teacher. On rare occasions, and in specific circumstances, your induction year can be extended, but this is not the norm. This 'make or break' situation makes your choice of school all the more important. Ensure you log on to the school's website and note the quality of induction provision offered by the school. If you know an NQT in the school, talk to him or her and ask about the quality of support offered to trainee teachers. You need to be aware that you are entitled to the following level of support from **all** schools as a matter of course:

- a reduced timetable – you should not teach any more than 90 per cent of a main-scale teacher's timetable
- an induction tutor
- a planned induction programme
- the right to observe experienced colleagues teaching
- the right to attend local authority-run courses
- the right to be observed and receive verbal and written feedback.

Another indicator of a suitable school is the 'Investors in People' award which is conferred on schools that prove they treat their staff with professional and personal respect. If this award has been given to a school then it is highly likely that you will be offered numerous opportunities for professional development.

One of the most important sources of information about the quality of a school can be found in the latest Ofsted report published on the school website and on the government website at www.ofsted.gov.uk. Close inspection of this data will inform you about: the behaviour of the children, the level of pastoral care and the quality of teaching and learning within the school. However, be extremely cautious when exploring these Ofsted reports, particularly as some will have been carried out a long time ago. You can use the Ofsted report to inform your decision in two ways: you can apply to a school that has obtained a successful report and capitalize upon all the good work that has gone on beforehand; or you could apply to a less successful school knowing that you will relish meeting the challenges.

32 Writing letters of application

The importance of writing a good letter of application should not be overestimated. This is particularly true in situations where supply exceeds demand. Even in situations where only one or two candidates have applied for a post, headteachers and governors may simply dismiss poorly written applications. It seems that many of them would prefer to wait until the right person comes along for the job rather than make an inappropriate appointment. Because this is going to be your first full-time teaching job, you will not be expected to write a long letter. As long as you have crafted your letter in an effective and efficient manner, keeping to a couple of sides of A4 should be sufficient. You need to be aware that there is a great deal of variation in terms of the paperwork required to make a job application. Some schools will also ask you to complete an application form in addition to a letter of application. Other schools will require a cv to support both of these. All the advice and guidance offered to you in Chapter 3 about completing application forms applies to this situation.

There are some general principles to consider when writing a letter of application for your first teaching job.

- It is absolutely vital that you make specific mention of those things you have been asked in the job description to include in your letter.
- You need to include your particular academic interests, achievements, personal qualities and skills, and make these relevant to the advertised position.
- State clearly what you can bring to the role for which you are applying.
- Without pontificating too much about this, you need to describe the educational principles that inform your teaching.
- Make it clear what additional things you can bring to the school. You may have particular sporting or drama skills which you will be able to offer. It could be that you used skills in your previous employment and that these are transferable to a number of school scenarios. In a highly competitive climate, schools will be looking for that little bit extra.

- It is important to get the tone of your letter right. Make sure that you are enthusiastic about the possibility of teaching at the school, about this specific post and about teaching in general. A good letter of application will be successful in conveying your values, beliefs, skills, qualities and personality to a headteacher, and in giving her an indication as to whether she might wish to work with you.
- Use examples of your teaching to illustrate your points.

Using the correct protocol

Although it is vital that letters of application show individuality and independence of thought, it is also very important that the correct protocol is followed. Failure to do so could seriously jeopardize your chance of an interview. With this is in mind, guidance is provided below for writing letters of application for a teaching post:

- Word-process your letter unless specifically asked not to. In order to avoid a cramped presentational style, use one and a half line spacing. You are also advised to think carefully about using an appropriate font. Times New Roman or Arial are often used.
- Make sure that your name and contact details have been included at the top of your letter of application (address, phone numbers and email address).
- Ensure that you have addressed the headteacher correctly (check on his or her status).
- Check your letter thoroughly for grammatical and spelling mistakes, and make sure that it reads fluently. Get your mentor, professional tutor or an English teacher to read it through.
- Use paragraphs and remember that each new idea should form a new paragraph.
- Ensure that your letter of application arrives on time even if you have to deliver it by hand.

Structure and content

When constructing your letter of application you need to think very carefully about the nature of your target audience. Be aware that headteachers and senior managers are extremely busy people and that they will not respond well to having to read and reread a poorly written letter of application. A good letter of application will tell the reader a lot about you. If your letter has a clear structure, is written with a real sense of flow and contains no grammatical or spelling errors, it will convey the message that you care about the job for which you are applying. It will also emphasize that you are likely to approach your professional tasks and dilemmas in a structured, logical and considered fashion. In short, it will show your ability to demonstrate 'joined-up thinking'. Conversely, if your letter of application is full of mistakes and is muddled in its presentation and style, then a very different message will be conveyed to the reader: that you are highly likely to adopt an unfocused approach to the professional scenarios presented to you. With this in mind, the following guidance on how to structure your letter of application is presented below.

Introductory paragraph

- Start your letter by referring to the post for which you are applying and by making reference to where and when the post was advertised. You also need to describe the nature of your university degree and state which college or university you are currently studying at.

Core

- In your second paragraph, make it clear why you want to work in this particular school. You need to impress upon the reader that you have carried out some research into the aims, ethos and academic performances of the school. Make it clear to the reader that you have read the contextual information sent to you by the school and make links between this and your experiences, qualities, skills and academic interests. For example, if maths is a priority for the school, and this is a particular strength of yours, make this clear and share what you could contribute.
- Although it is important not to be sycophantic, you do need to convey to the reader that the information gleaned from your research has greatly impressed you and that it has made you excited about the possibility of working at this particular school. When applying to a good school, introduce the phrase 'I would enjoy the challenge of working in a school with such high standards' into your text.

  That's all well and good if you are applying to a successful school. However, which approach should you adopt if you are applying to a school that is well down the league-table? Our advice here would be to display a recognition and understanding of the external factors that can affect a child's performance at school and to say how much you would relish working towards raising the standards of those children from disadvantaged backgrounds.
- In your third paragraph, you need to highlight your particular academic strengths, interests and personal qualities. However, remember to link

these strongly with the requirements of the advertised post. For example, if the post requires the successful candidate to teach Year 3 then this would be the place to mention that you had a successful practice with a Year 3/4 class. If the school want someone with an interest in ICT, you could outline the ways you have used this successfully in a practice. This is also the place to outline your teaching philosophy and make strong links between this and the advertised post. For example, if you believe very strongly in collaborative working, you might link this to the fact that the school has a small team of staff who work closely together. Continue in this vein to discuss how your teaching is informed by your beliefs and/or by theoretical approaches towards your subject.

- In paragraph four, you need to convey to the reader that you are more than just a class teacher. At this point, indicate the extra-curricular activities you could offer the school. If you can identify links between the advertised post and your outside interests then do so. For example, you could write about your willingness to set up an after-school science club for the keen scientists or, if you have contacts from your previous job as a sports coach, you could talk about using possible contacts you have established. Have a look at the school's extra-curricular programme and identify whether there any gaps which you could fill.

- Paragraph five could see you describing your pre-training experiences with children and/or the particular areas of success within your training. Again, it is important to link these with the advertised post and not simply to present them in a list-type fashion. If these experiences have helped to develop your organizational skills or your ability to interact with children, then describe the positive impact this could have for you in the school should your application be successful. Remember to stress how much you enjoy working with young people and to describe the satisfaction you gain from helping them to progress.

Concluding paragraph

- If your letter is not accompanied by an application form, then furnish the school with the names and contact details of your referees. You need to end your letter with a concluding sentence that leaves the reader with a positive feeling about your application. Conclude your letter by writing something along the following lines:

Example 1

I see the advertised post as being a stimulating and challenging opportunity to develop my teaching skills. Should my application be successful, I would relish working within a school which has such a good team spirit and which offers so many opportunities for professional development.

Example 2

In conclusion, I would hope to add to the pool of expertise and excellent reputation of Y school through my leadership skills, innovative teaching and infectious enthusiasm. I would look forward to teaching in a school in which Ofsted has described behaviour as being 'very good' and where achievement is both recognized and rewarded.

Example 3

In conclusion, I believe that my experience, energy and drive make me an excellent candidate for the post being offered.

Mail-shot letters

There will inevitably be a number of you who will not have been offered jobs by the end of the third term. You are strongly advised to adopt a proactive approach towards the application process. In other words, write to a selected number of schools, furnishing them with relevant details and informing them of your current availability. It is possible that schools may have only just been informed that a member of staff is leaving. Some trainees do gain their first teaching post by carrying out a mail-shot of local schools and responding to the headteacher's invitation to come in to have a chat.

Many of the rules that apply when completing a general letter of application are similar to those required when responding to specifically advertised posts. However, in addition to furnishing the school with details of your teaching expertise, you need to stress your flexibility and your willingness to get involved in other areas of school life.

The benefits of being proactive in the application process are twofold. Providing your letter of application and cv are faultless, headteachers are highly likely to be extremely impressed by your ability to display drive and initiative. Second, at a time when increasing anxiety about not having a job is likely to affect the quality of your teaching, self-esteem and your interaction with staff and children, this is a good way of gaining some psychological control over your professional life. An example of a mail-shot letter of application is shown opposite.

Mr Dai Lemmer
5 Employment Chase
Barking
Essex
BA3 T11
Tel: 01122 321789
e: dl@asi.net

Mrs I.M. Hopeful
Headteacher
Beech Field Primary School
Tillett
Herts
TI1 4SS   12 January 20__

Dear Mrs Hopeful

I am a teacher trainee currently in the third term of my PGCE course at the University of Bradfield and am now beginning to seek employment for my induction year and beyond. Rather than simply waiting for opportunities to arise, I felt that it would be apposite to make a general application to your school in the hope that you may have a suitable vacancy.

I have looked at your school website and carried out some research into the academic and social aspects of life at Beech Field Primary School. My research indicates that the high degree of academic success enjoyed by the school is the result of a combination of excellent subject expertise and an extremely caring and proactive staff. The chance to work in a school that enjoys such a grand reputation among parents and in a local authority which offers excellent support has provided the motivation for this application. The location is perfect for me, as my partner has already secured a teaching post in a neighbouring school.

You will note from my cv that should an NQT post in Key Stage 2 arise, I would be well qualified to make an application. I am particularly proud of the 2:1 I achieved in my degree from the University of Bradfield. Although I have not yet finished my PGCE course, I have provided my 'Good' teaching-practice reports for my first two practices and I am confident that should you require evidence of my capabilities, these will show that I am making very good progress. I anticipate securing QTS status (with the associated PGCE qualification) in June.

I have been fully committed to the idea of teaching for a number of years. My experience of working with young people, in three different practice schools, has strengthened my determination to teach. I enjoy the challenge of motivating reluctant learners alongside those who are gifted and highly motivated. My first teaching placement allowed me to work with a number of children who exhibited a range of behavioural problems. In observing experienced colleagues, I soon recognized the importance of setting expectations, and using praise and sanctions when necessary. I also learned that children will work for you if you exhibit warmth and commitment to them. In my current placement, I was pleased to be asked to work with a small number of children who are on the school's gifted and talented register. I found this to be particularly rewarding as it challenged me to develop my subject knowledge still further.

Those who know me well recognize a steely determination to succeed alongside a willingness to be part of a team. Although I may lack experience, I am committed and enthusiastic, and keen to take part in extra–curricular activities and whole-school events. I note that Beech Field School has a reputation for the quality of its drama productions. While at university, I was an active member of the dramatic society and would be more than willing to offer my services in school productions.

The chance to work in your school is an exciting one. I would be happy to expand on my aspirations in an interview, should you decide to offer me this opportunity.

Yours sincerely

Dai Lemmer

Preparing for your NQT selection day

33

On the assumption that at least one of your letters has 'hit the spot' and that you have been called to interview, we would like to offer you some guidance on how to prepare for the selection day. You will note that we have again used the term 'selection day' rather than 'interview day' because, as was the case with your training-provider selection day, the interview itself may form only one part of the selection process. You may have the opportunity to apply to a local authority 'pool' where you attend one interview with a panel of headteachers and advisers. You will then receive an interview grade which is released to all schools looking for an NQT. They may then call you directly and offer you the chance of an informal chat, which may be followed by a job offer. This has the great advantage of only having to attend one formal interview. However, if your pool interview does not go well, you are then stuck with your grade.

If you do not or cannot apply within this system, you may have to go to interview at each school offering a job. In this case, it is highly likely that you will have to teach either a full lesson or at least a part lesson, and that you will be expected to meet and interact with a group of staff and/or children. The main message we want to convey to you at this point is that the selection procedure is very much a two-way process. Although it is vital for you to do everything you can to make a good impression on the school, the converse also applies. The school needs to make an impression on you. If you are fortunate enough to have been called for interview, we would strongly advise that you visit the school prior to your selection day to meet with the headteacher and to take the opportunity to make a tour of the school. By doing this, both parties will have an opportunity to 'size each other up'.

When you visit the school make sure you dress appropriately. Men need to wear a suit or at the very least a smart jacket and trousers. Women should wear a suit, smart dress or jacket with trousers or skirt. Make sure that you at least know the name of the headteacher before you arrive at the school. Be sure to address members of staff formally unless invited to use their first names.

Bearing in mind that the purpose of your visit is to ascertain whether this is the right headteacher and school for you, you need to have a number of questions in mind to ask yourself during the day. In preparation for this visit, you could reread the section on the 'School Ethos' found in Chapter 3, as this will help you to make a decision as to whether the culture of the school is to your liking. In addition to this input, a list of specific questions, that you may want to think about on the day is included below:

- Is the headteacher friendly and approachable? Does he make you feel important and comfortable?
- How well does the headteacher interact with children and/or other staff? Does he show respect to these people?
- Do the school staff appear to be friendly and happy in their work?
- Can you identify any specific staff with likeminded views to you?
- What is the rate of staff turnover? (This may be tricky to find out!)
- Are most of the children generally on-task and well-behaved in their lessons?
- What is corridor and playground behaviour like?
- What is the quality of teacher/child relationships in the school?
- Would your teaching style and approach be welcomed in the school?
- What induction training and professional development opportunities exist for your NQT year and beyond?
- What is the physical environment of the school like?
- To what extent does the school reflect and respect different cultures?

Ideally, you need to discuss your visit with someone who has a experience of teaching in a number of schools, but if this is not possible then take every opportunity to discuss the situation with a friend or family member. Very often just being able to articulate your thoughts to another person is enough to help you to make your decision.

Making an initial impression

34

Whatever the outcome of your interview, you need to hold your head up high in the knowledge that you have done extremely well to get this far. Headteachers are pretty ruthless in weeding out substandard application forms/letters, so you must be doing something right if you have been called for interview.

Your assessment basically begins from the time when you first start to 'meet and greet' people. Be fully aware that no matter how pleasant members of staff are towards you, they will inevitably be making judgements about whether they feel they could work alongside you. To this end, therefore, make sure that you follow the same advice offered to you about your pre-interview visits. Some schools ask their children to take candidates on a tour of the building and/or to hold a discussion forum. It is highly likely that these children will be asked to give their opinion of you as a potential teacher at the school. Our advice here is for you to interact as much as possible with these children, making sure that you not only ask questions about the school but also about these young people themselves. Having said this, ensure that you are also very careful not to pry and not to dominate any of the sessions. You may be unfortunate enough to have a domineering candidate alongside you on the selection day. You know the type: they know best; they have been everywhere; they've done everything; seen everything. Whatever you do, do not try to compete with these people. Our advice here would be to 'keep your dignity', and simply let them get on with it. Staff and children alike are very quick to see through people like this and it is highly likely that they will be weeded out early on in the selection process.

35 Teaching your specimen lesson

It is now common practice for schools to ask prospective NQT candidates to teach either a full lesson or a part lesson on the selection/interview day. This lesson is likely to be observed by the headteacher or deputy headteacher, or an experienced practitioner. Their observation reports will be fed back to the interview panel and may provide a focus for discussion. Whether you are successful or not in landing the job, you should expect to receive feedback on how your lesson went.

Although this can be quite a daunting experience, you need to treat this lesson observation as a gateway of opportunity, a chance to show what you can really do. No school is going to give you a really challenging class to teach, so although you need to remember your classroom management strategies, these should not provide the main focus for your planning. You will note that we have titled this chapter 'Teaching your specimen lesson' and that is precisely what you will be doing. In a period of between 20 and 30 minutes you have to do everything you can to convince the school that you have got what it takes to join their teaching staff. You are strongly advised to plan this lesson with military precision and leave nothing to chance. In order to help you to do this there are some suggestions.

Top tips for teaching your specimen lesson

- Find out about the children in the class beforehand if you can. Make a note of any with special educational needs or for whom English is an additional language.
- If you are given a choice, select a topic which you can make highly relevant to your class and choose something that you know they will be really interested in. If you have been allocated a specific topic to teach, then do everything you can to make this relevant to their experiences.
- Plan your lesson in accordance with the guidance offered in Chapter 7. Ensure that your lesson has a starter, core and plenary. Although you will not have first-hand knowledge of the children, offer opportunities for differentiation by outcome. Bearing in mind the limited time available,

make sure that you include timing slots in your plan and that you keep to them. Do not let your lesson overrun, as doing so will disadvantage the other candidates or you may simply be stopped mid-flow.

- This is your chance to demonstrate to the observer that you have a full understanding of the planning process. Find out who will be observing you and provide her with a lesson plan.

- Make sure that you launch your lesson by introducing yourself and by giving your children a brief outline of your expectations as far as their behaviour and work ethic are concerned. Doing this will raise your status with the class and will indicate to the observer that this is what you routinely practise. Introduce the learning objective.

- Produce a range of resources and activities for the lesson, taking into account the need to cater for visual, auditory and kinaesthetic learners wherever possible.

- Be sure to carry out some monitoring and assessment of children's learning during the lesson and in the plenary session. You could even set up a simple peer-assessment activity. The very least you need to do is to carry out a question-and-answer session to assess whether the learning objectives have been realized. In the spirit of true inclusivity, make sure that you do everything you can to involve and assess the learning of the least and most able in the class.

- Be sure to thank the children for their attention at the end of the lesson and tell them how much you have enjoyed the experience.

- While you are teaching your lesson, make a mental note of what you feel is going well and what you would do differently should you be given the opportunity to teach the same lesson again. You may be asked a question about the quality of your lesson in your interview, so be prepared to demonstrate your ability to reflect and evaluate.

35 The interview

Although all schools differ, it is highly likely that your interview panel will consist of the headteacher, a school governor and maybe an adviser. Because of the extremely mixed nature of the panel, you can expect a wide range of questions to be asked. In addition to the teaching and learning aspect of the interview, the panel will also be looking very closely at your interpersonal and intrapersonal skills. When you enter the room, smile and greet each member of the interview panel warmly, make eye contact with each person and shake their hands firmly.

Some interviews are conducted in a very formal manner while others are very relaxed. Be prepared for anything! If the interview follows on from the specimen lesson, be prepared to answer questions that will require you to offer an evaluation of your lesson. Make sure that you also know your application form and letter really well, as you could be asked to expand upon a point you made. Each interviewer will have a specific brief. Depending upon their specific area of expertise, different panel members will ask questions designed to find out about

- you as a person
- your views on the purpose of schooling and education
- how enthusiastic you are about teaching in general and about teaching at this specific school
- the level of your subject knowledge and expertise
- the quality of your planning and organization
- the nature and quality of your training
- how you can use your skills and personal qualities to good effect in this post
- how reflective and evaluative you are
- how you are likely to respond to specific circumstances.

Because of the unpredictable nature of the interview process, it is not possible for us to furnish you with a finite list of interview questions, but some possible ones have been included in Figure 35.1.

The school governor

- Why do you want to teach in this school?
- How well do you think your ITT course has prepared you for this post?
- What support will you require in your first year of teaching?
- Where do you see yourself professionally in five years' time?
- How might you include classroom assistants in your lesson-planning?
- How would you plan for the inclusion of children who have a limited or no command of spoken English?
- How would you deal with challenging behaviour in your class?
- How would you deal with bullying?

The headteacher

- If I came into your classroom, how would I know the children were learning?
- What has impressed you about this school and what has disappointed you?
- What skills and personal qualities do you feel you can bring to this post?
- What evidence do you have to show that you are a team-player?
- In addition to your work in the classroom, what else can you offer the school?
- We organize our teaching with Years 3 and 4 into sets for literacy and numeracy. How do you feel about this?
- What would you do if a parent complained to you that her child was bored in your lessons?

The Adviser

- Why do you want to teach Year 3?
- What are the characteristics of an excellent lesson?
- Give me an example of a recent lesson that you think has gone well. Explain why.
- Give me an example of a recent lesson that disappointed you. What went wrong and what would you do in the future?
- What strategies would you use when teaching X (a challenging topic)?
- What would you say to a child who asks you a subject-related question which you are unable to answer?

Table 35.1 Potential interview questions

As we have already noted earlier in this chapter, it is not possible to second guess an interview panel, or to provide a list of definitive questions you will be asked on the day. Nor is it likely that members of the panel will ask their questions using exactly the same phraseology presented to you in this chapter. Although we hope that the range of questions provided for you will go some way to supporting you on the big day, you are nevertheless, going to have to be extremely flexible and to 'think on your feet' when responding to questions asked by the panel. There is also great a deal of truth in the phrase 'practice makes perfect', and we strongly recommend that you ask your professional tutor and mentor to give you a mock interview before you attend your selection days. If you require further support on the interview process then we highly recommend the following website: www.interviewstuff.com/

Career entry and development profile 37

Towards the end of your training you will be asked to complete a career entry and development profile (CEDP), which is designed to help you think about your professional development in the latter stages of your ITT training and throughout your induction year. The profile process has been designed to encourage you to reflect on your own teaching and professional development and is structured around three transition points.

Transition point one

As your initial teacher-training course draws to a close, you will be given the opportunity to reflect on your professional development, your strengths and developmental needs, and be encouraged to start thinking about your aspirations for your induction year. Although you will work with your mentor and tutor on this document, you need to be fully aware that it is your responsibility to record your own responses to the CEDP prompt questions provided.

Transition point two

At the beginning of your induction year, you will be asked to meet with your induction tutor and talk through your priorities for induction. Part of the discussion will focus on how you can build upon the targets you set yourself at the end of your training, and how your induction tutors can use the CEDP to plan and review your support programme in your NQT year.

Transition point three

Towards the end of your induction year, you will be supported by your induction tutor to look back on your induction period to reflect on your progress during the year and to think about your aspirations for your continuing professional development (CPD).

Our underlying purpose in Part 7 has been to highlight the need for you to take control of your own professional future. Throughout this section we have constantly urged you not to sit back and wait for opportunities to arise, but to adopt a proactive approach towards the application and selection process. We live in a highly competitive world and teaching is a reflection of this. Schools are looking for innovative, proactive trainees who have a clear vision of the future and who are able to show personal initiative and drive.

Conclusion

We are both hopeful and confident that this handbook will have provided you with guidance and advice on most of the issues that are likely to arise during your training. However, it would be totally unrealistic to have covered every professional scenario that is likely to crop up in every primary school across the country. Each school differs in its ethos, culture and way of doing things. Each school has a bank of employees who are unique both in terms of their corporate characteristics and in the individual personalities of those who work there. Having said this, there are some relatively predictable similarities in the scenarios presented to trainees during their school practices: we have tried to cover most of these. The guidance offered in this handbook has generally been presented in a chronological manner in order to make it easy for you to identify your needs at any given point during your training. In order to add further transparency to the process we have linked much of the advice and guidance offered to the relevant QTS standards. By doing this we hope to aid you in gathering the evidence required to move you towards qualified teacher status.

So, where do you go from here? On the assumption that you have acted upon the advice and guidance offered to you within this handbook, and that you have landed yourself a job for your NQT year, we would like to congratulate you on reaching your initial destination. Enjoy the moment but please be fully aware that you are about to start yet another journey: that of your induction year. Do not forget all you have learned and do not rest on your laurels. We haven't! Ensure that you seize every professional development opportunity offered to you. Approach your induction year, and every year thereafter, with enthusiasm, diligence and above all, reflectivity. Providing that you do this, we are convinced that you will enjoy a long, fruitful and enjoyable career.

> He who dares to teach must never cease to learn.
>
> (Anonymous)

Appendix 1

Professional standards for qualified teacher status

Professional attributes

Relationships with children and young people

Q1 Have high expectations of children and young people including a commitment to ensuring that they can achieve their full educational potential and to establishing fair, respectful, trusting, supportive and constructive relationships with them.

Q2 Demonstrate the positive values, attitudes and behaviour they expect from children and young people.

Frameworks

Q3(a) Be aware of the professional duties of teachers and the statutory framework within which they work.

(b) Be aware of the policies and practices of the workplace and share in collective responsibility for their implementation.

Communicating and working with others

Q4 Communicate effectively with children, young people, colleagues, parents and carers.

Q5 Recognize and respect the contribution that colleagues, parents and carers can make to the development and well-being of children and young people and to raising their levels of attainment.

Q6 Have a commitment to collaboration and cooperative working.

Personal professional development

Q7(a) Reflect on and improve their practice, and take responsibility for identifying and meeting their developing professional needs.

(b) Identify priorities for their early professional development in the context of induction.

Q8 Have a creative and constructively critical approach towards innovation, being prepared to adapt their practice where benefits and improvements are identified.

Q9 Act upon advice and feedback and be open to coaching and mentoring.

Professional knowledge and understanding

Teaching and learning

Q10 Have a knowledge and understanding of a range of teaching, learning and behaviour-management strategies and know how to use and adapt them, including how to personalize learning and provide opportunities for all learners to achieve their potential.

Assessment and monitoring

Q11 Know the assessment requirements and arrangements for the subjects/ curriculum areas in the age-ranges they are trained to teach, including those relating to public examinations and qualifications.

Q12 Know a range of approaches to assessment, including the importance of formative assessment.

Q13 Know how to use local and national statistical information to evaluate the effectiveness of their teaching, to monitor the progress of those they teach and to raise levels of attainment.

Subjects and curriculum

Q14 Have a secure knowledge and understanding of their subjects/curriculum areas and related pedagogy to enable them to teach effectively across the age and ability range for which they are trained.

Q15 Know and understand the relevant statutory and non-statutory curricula, frameworks, including those provided through the National Strategies, for their subjects/curriculum areas, and other relevant initiatives applicable to the age and ability range for which they are trained.

Literacy, numeracy and ICT

Have passed the professional skills tests in numeracy, literacy and information and communication technology (ICT).

Q17 Know how to use skills in literacy, numeracy and ICT to support their teaching and wider professional activities.

Achievement and diversity

Q18 Understand how children and young people develop and that the progress and well-being of learners are affected by a range of developmental, social, religious, ethnic, cultural and linguistic influences.

Q19 Know how to make effective personalized provision for those they teach, including those for whom English is an additional language or who have special educational needs or disabilities, and how to take practical account of diversity and promote equality and inclusion in their teaching.

Q20 Know and understand the roles of colleagues with specific responsibilities, including those with responsibility for learners with special educational needs and disabilities and other individual learning needs.

Health and well-being

Q21(a) Be aware of current legal requirements, national policies and guidance on the safeguarding and promotion of the well-being of children and young people.

(b) Know how to identify and support children and young people whose progress, development or well-being is affected by changes or difficulties in their personal circumstances, and when to refer them to colleagues for specialist support.

Professional skills

Planning

Q22 Plan for progression across the age and ability range for which they are trained, designing effective learning sequences within lessons and across series of lessons and demonstrating secure subject/curriculum knowledge.

Q23 Design opportunities for learners to develop their literacy, numeracy and ICT skills.

Q24 Plan homework or other out-of-class work to sustain learners' progress and to extend and consolidate their learning.

Teaching

Q25 Teach lessons and sequences of lessons across the age and ability range for which they are trained in which they:

(a) use a range of teaching strategies and resources, including e-learning, taking practical account of diversity and promoting equality and inclusion;

(b) build on prior knowledge, develop concepts and processes, enable learners to apply new knowledge, understanding and skills and meet learning objectives;

(c) adapt their language to suit the learners they teach, introducing new ideas and concepts clearly, and using explanations, questions, discussions and plenaries effectively;

(d) manage the learning of individuals, groups and whole classes, modifying their teaching to suit the stage of the lesson.

Assessing, monitoring and giving feedback

Q26(a) Make effective use of a range of assessment, monitoring and recording strategies.

(b) Assess the learning needs of those they teach in order to set challenging learning objectives.

Q27 Provide timely, accurate and constructive feedback on learners' attainment, progress and areas for development.

Q28 Support and guide learners to reflect on their learning, identify the progress they have made and identify their emerging learning needs.

Reviewing teaching and learning

Q29 Evaluate the impact of their teaching on the progress of all learners, and modify their planning and classroom practice where necessary.

Learning environment

Q30 Establish a purposeful and safe learning environment conducive to learning and identify opportunities for learners to learn in out of school contexts.

Q31 Establish a clear framework for classroom discipline to manage learners' behaviour constructively and promote their self-control and independence.

Team working and collaboration

Q32 Work as a team member and identify opportunities for working with colleagues, sharing the development of effective practice with them.

Q33 Ensure that colleagues working with them are appropriately involved in supporting learning and understand the roles they are expected to fulfil.

Appendix 2

Level descriptors for English

Speaking

QCA Level	QCA/EAL statement	What the pupil can do at this level	Teacher strategies to help pupils move on
Pre Step 1		• May use single words • Will gesture or use L1 to convey meaning • Likely to be in the 'silent period'	• Be welcoming • Make eye contact • Include pupils in a group • Provide visual clues
Step 1	Pupils echo words and expressions drawn from classroom routines and social interactions to communicate meaning. They express some basic needs, using single words or phrases in English.	• Understands a little, but could still be in 'silent period' • Can respond to familiar questions and instructions using single words, short phrases, gestures or L1 • Can ask for help using single words • Can name familiar classroom objects and equipment	• Include pupil in all activities, but do not try to force her to speak • Use natural English in short, simple phrases and sentences • Use closed questions with contextual support • Give time for answers • Allow other pupils who speak the same language to support responses
Step 2	Pupils copy speech that has been modelled. In their speech they show some control of English word-order and their pronunciation is generally intelligible.	• Can use a small range of familiar phrases to communicate needs and ideas/meaning • Beginning to use English in small group setting in classroom activities • Shows some control of English word-order and pronunciation in short utterances • Will use repetition to extend use of English	• Model key words and phrases and encourage other pupils to do the same • Create opportunities to speak in carefully structured situations

QCA Level	QCA/EAL statement	What the pupil can do at this level	Teacher strategies to help pupils move on
Level 1 Threshold (L1T)	Pupils speak about matters of immediate interest in familiar settings. They convey meaning through talk and gesture and can extend what they say with support. Their speech is sometimes grammatically incomplete at word and phrase level.	• Can convey meaning and express needs using two or three word phrases • With support, will make contributions to group/class discussion • Can speak more fluently with friends in everyday situations • Is exploring grammatical structures to generate meaningful sentences, but although the meaning is clear, the grammar will sometimes not be appropriate	• Respond positively to contributions • Model language by 'echoing' the pupil's utterances, using the appropriate grammar • Be aware that conversational fluency comes a long time before fluency in academic English

Level 1 Secure (L1S)	Pupils speak about matters of interest to a range of listeners and begin to develop connected utterances. What they say shows some grammatical complexity in expressing relationships between ideas and sequences of events. Pupils convey meaning, sustaining their contributions and listeners' interest.	• Is beginning to be able to express the logical relationships between ideas using features of language such as connectives
		• Can sustain meaning and keep the listener's interest, often by using voice and gesture
			• Opportunities for group and pair discussion
			• Encourage pupil to develop spoken ideas by:
			  – giving thinking time
			  – asking questions
			  – suggesting connectives
			  – (because, although, etc.)
			• Sometimes encourage the use of writing to organize ideas before discussion, e.g. flow-charts, grids, mind-maps
			• Give opportunities for group presentations where individual bilingual pupils can be supported by others

Listening

QCA Level	QCA/EAL statement	What the pupil can do at this level	Teacher strategies to help pupils move on
Pre Step 1		• Understands a little • May join in activities • Understands and responds in L1 • Uses visual clues for meaning • Can respond non-verbally to everyday expressions, e.g. greetings • May use gestures to indicate active listening	• Be welcoming • Make eye contact • Include pupils in a group • Provide visual clues
Step 1	Pupils listen attentively for a short time. They use non-verbal gestures to respond to greetings and questions about themselves and they follow simple instructions based on the routines of the classroom.	• Relies on visual cues for meaning with L1 support may join in classroom activities • Will respond positively to friendly approaches from peers • Participates as a listener in group activities • Can name familiar class objects/equipment • Can listen attentively for a short time • Can understand and follow familiar instructions	• Mix activities • Keep teacher presentations short • Keep to familiar classroom routines • Structure lessons to include suitable activities, e.g. matching, labelling • Give opportunities for listening in small groups
Step 2	Pupils understand simple conversational English. They listen and respond to the gist of general explanations by the teacher where language is supported by non-verbal cues, including illustrations.	• Understands familiar conversational phrases • Can follow narrative expressed through spoken and visual material • Understands simple ideas or explanations with help of mime, gesture or pictures • Listens and responds to paired/group discussion	• Use visuals/practicals/demonstrations to support teacher talk • Allow time for pupil to listen to and question a friend who speaks the same language • Refer to key visual while explaining

QCA Level	QCA/EAL statement	What the pupil can do at this level	Teacher strategies to help pupils move on
Level 1 Threshold (L1T)	With support, pupils understand and respond appropriately to straightforward comment or instruction addressed to them. They listen attentively to a range of speakers, including teacher presentation to the whole class.	• Listens well but needs to discuss new ideas to help understanding • Can listen attentively to the class teacher or to other pupils • Responds to straightforward instructions	• Be aware that attentive listening does not necessarily mean understanding • Support for key words using visuals • List key words before lesson for support staff or use a bilingual dictionary where appropriate • Pre-teach key words (through starters, using support staff, etc.)
Level 1 Secure (L1S)	In familiar contexts, pupils follow what others say about what they are doing and thinking. They listen with understanding to sequences of instructions and usually respond appropriately in conversation.	• Can understand most classroom interactions and explanations with visual or other support • Will follow familiar instructions and respond appropriately, but may not understand unfamiliar words or idioms.	• Be aware that the pupil will not be familiar with many words that the other pupils know • Continue to support key words using visuals • Approach abstract ideas through concrete examples or L1

Reading

NB: these steps and levels apply to pupils who are not securely literate in their first language

QCA Level	QCA/EAL statement	What the pupil can do at this level	Teacher strategies to help pupils move on
Pre Step 1		• Not securely literate in the home language and will take more time to learn to read in English because he needs knowledge of English to use reading for meaning strategies	• Model reading behaviour, e.g. locating title, reading from left to right, using picture clues to predict, etc.
Step 1	Pupils participate in reading activities. They know that in English print is read from left to right and from top to bottom. They recognize their names and familiar words and identify some letters of the alphabet by shape and sound.	• May use L1 in accessing English text • Will recognize his name and some other familiar words, e.g. from advertising • Is starting to become familiar with the shape and sound of letters of the alphabet	• Encourage use of L1, especially for exploring ideas • Pupils will be unfamiliar with the names of letters of the alphabet • Use group/shared/paired reading • Keep texts short and accessible • Introduce and explain using words and pictures, labelling, simple sequencing with visuals
Step 2	Pupils begin to associate with letters in English to predict what the text will be about. They read words and phrases that they have learned in different curriculum areas. With support they can follow a text read aloud.	• Making connections between English sounds and letters • Begins to read some simple words/signs/labels around classroom/school • Can read simple texts with repeating language and structure • Predicts story/events of a text using visual cues/ discussion • Can read back own writing scribed by an adult • May be able to decode more than he can understand	• Encourage use of contextual and visual clues • Support the reading of even very short texts using other pupils, support staff, discussion or L1 • Use pupil's own writing as familiar text to read • Use talking books

QCA Level	QCA/EAL statement	What the pupil can do at this level	Teacher strategies to help pupils move on
Level 1 Threshold (L1T)	Pupils can read a range of familiar words and identify initial and final sounds in unfamiliar words. With support, they can establish meaning when reading aloud phrases or simple sentences and use contextual clues to gain understanding. They respond to ideas in poems, stories and non-fiction.	• Recognizes and knows the sound of most letters of the alphabet • Has developed a sight vocabulary of some common words and those used in the curriculum • Reads aloud known and predictable texts • Decodes unknown words using contextual and pictorial cues • Can demonstrate an understanding of what is being read • Can read and understand simple text with support	• Introduce and explain active reading strategies – underlining, colour-coding, transferring words into a grid, annotating pictures, etc. • Activate prior knowledge and thinking as a way into a text • Use group and paired activities to support reading • Avoid silent reading and use talk to support understanding
Level 1 Secure (L1S)	Pupils use their knowledge of letters, sounds and words to establish meaning when reading familiar texts aloud, sometimes with prompting. They comment on events or ideas in poems, stories and non-fiction.	• Increased sight vocabulary of commonly used words in different contexts • Can read aloud using knowledge of sounds and letter (but may not understand) • Can read complex known English texts but needs support with unfamiliar text, idioms and grammar • Responds to text expressing personal views, answering factual questions • With support can infer meaning	• Make talking books with pupils • Always discuss topic before reading • Active interaction with text • Choose text with visual clues • Let pupil know the purpose of the reading task • Teach pupils how to navigate non-fiction text (blocks of text, etc.) • Explain how to read diagrams, graphs, grids, etc.

Writing

NB: These steps and levels apply to pupils who are not securely literate in their first language.

QCA Level	QCA/EAL statement	What the pupil can do at this level	Teacher strategies to help pupils move on
Pre Step 1		• Not securely literate in the home language and will take more time to learn to write in English • Can use pictures to convey meaning • Can understand that written scripts convey meaning • Can hold and use a pencil appropriately • Can copy recognizable English symbols	• Model writing behaviour, e.g. writing from left to right, keeping to the line, shaping letters, and support correct use of pen and pencil • Speaking and listening are essential before any writing, to give meaning to the task • Encourage use of pictures to convey meaning • Use picture annotation
Step 1	Pupils use English letter and letter-like forms to convey meaning. They copy or write their names and familiar words and write from left to right.	• Can form some letters from memory • Can write own name and some other familiar words • Can write some initial sounds • Can relate some English sounds to the written form	• Generate text orally • Support writing of single words and short, simple phrases • Confine initial writing to lower case • Encourage use of L1, especially if L1 is written in Roman script • Using single words and phrases in L1 helps to establish the concept of sound-letter relationship
Step 2	Pupils attempt to express meaning through writing supported by oral work or pictures. Generally their writing is intelligible to themselves and a familiar reader and shows some knowledge of sound and letter patterns in English spelling.	• Writing stems from oral rehearsal and pictorial support (may also want to practise in L1) • Writing is legible to themselves and familiar readers • Can write final sounds • Will attempt to read back own writing • In discussing own written text, will be able to explain more than he can write	• Use grids, labelling, captioning, etc. • Use shared writing with peer or adult support • Encourage pupil to dictate text to scribe and then to reread text with scribe

QCA Level	QCA/EAL statement	What the pupil can do at this level	Teacher strategies to help pupils move on
Level 1 Threshold (L1T)	Pupils produce recognizable letters and words in texts, which convey meaning and show some knowledge of English sentence division and word-order. Most commonly used letters are correctly shaped, but may be inconsistent in their size and orientation.	• Writes letters and words increasingly legibly • Write independently and convey meaning through recognizable words, phrases and sentences but spelling and sentence structure are irregular	• Respond to the meaning of the pupil writing, not the form • Encourage pupils to read own writing aloud and help them self-correct orally • Do not over correct • Use sentence starters and simple writing frames to support
Level 1 Secure (L1S)	Pupils use phrases and longer statements to convey ideas to the reader, making use of full stops and capital letters. Some grammatical patterns are irregular and pupils' grasp of English sounds and how they are written is not secure. Letters are usually clearly shaped and correctly orientated.	• Begin to use simple punctuation: full stops capital letters • Write increasingly legibly with letters clearly shaped and correctly orientated and appropriate spacing between words • Spell familiar and CVC words correctly • Writing demonstrates more complex ideas in sequences of events	• Scaffold writing with group activities and oral rehearsal • Use grids, flow-charts, etc. to help structure writing • Let pupils read back own writing and discuss the ideas with supporting adult in English or L1 if preferred • Model correct grammatical expression in responses to work whilst still focusing on content before form (this is important at all levels)

Level 2

Skill	QCA/EAL statement	What the pupil can do at this level	Teacher strategies to help pupils move on

Speaking and Listening	Pupils begin to show confidence in talking and listening, particularly where the topic interest them. On occasions, they show awareness of the needs of the listener by including relevant detail. In developing and explaining their ideas they speak clearly and use a growing vocabulary. They usually listen carefully and respond with increasing appropriateness to what others say.
	
	They are beginning to be aware that in some situations a more formal vocabulary and tone of voice are used.
		• Beginning to show confidence in speaking to convey meaning. This could be by using familiar language in new contexts
		• Uses interactions to extend range of speaking style
		• In these interactions, shows awareness by responding to both verbal and non-verbal clues
		• Uses a wider range of vocabulary, including subject-specific vocabulary
		• Beginning to use a wider range of strategies, both verbal and non-verbal, for checking understanding
		• Beginning to be aware of change of register in different situations although social speech will be ahead of speech for learning
			• Continue to respond positively and constructively
			• Avoid seeming to correct even when grammar and/or vocabulary is not entirely appropriate
			• Responses should include:
			  – acknowledging understanding
			  – continuing dialogue
			  – modelling appropriate language in context
			• Provide opportunities for small-group and one-to-one interaction
			• Appropriate register should be made explicit and discussed

Reading	Pupils' reading of simple texts shows understanding and is generally accurate. They express opinions about major events or ideas in stories, poems and non-fiction. They use more than one strategy such as phonic, graphic, syntactic, and contextual, in reading unfamiliar words and establishing meaning.	• Beginning to read a variety of fiction and non-fiction without support • Can sustain accurate, independent reading over short passages of text • In discussion, gives views on some main points of the text • When subject matter is familiar, can use a variety of strategies to make sense of the text and self-correct	• Occasionally discuss methods of reading for understanding, e.g. 'How did you work out what it meant?' • Continue to support reading by activating prior knowledge and thinking • Continue to support understanding with visuals • Continue to use text for a clear purpose (active reading)

Skill	QCA/EAL statement	What the pupil can do at this level	Teacher strategies to help pupils move on
Writing	Pupils' writing communicates meaning in both narrative and non-narrative forms, using appropriate and interesting vocabulary, and showing some awareness of the reader. Ideas are developed in a sequence of sentences, sometimes demarcated by capital letters and full stops. Simple monosyllabic words are usually spelled correctly, and where there are inaccuracies the alternative is phonetically plausible.	• Write accurately enough for an outside reader to understand • Write for different purposes, although may produce writing more based on speech than written models • Link ideas together within a text • Spell simple words correctly and use phonetically plausible spelling for other words • Use capital letters and full stops • Use more complex or lengthy sentences although grammatical construction may show evidence of EAL • Use a wider vocabulary • Will be able to structure a chronologically organized text more easily than other types of text	• Teach how to use a simple thesaurus (e.g. *Usborne's Illustrated*) • Encourage pupils to use or compile a subject-specific glossary • Support pupils in structuring non-narrative text through discussion and use of simple writing-frames • Make explicit and discuss different forms of writing (e.g. story, report, explanation, instructions, etc.)

Level 3

Skill	QCA/EAL statement	What the pupil can do at this level	Teacher strategies to help pupils move on
Speaking and listening	Pupils talk and listen confidently in different contexts, exploring and communicating ideas. In discussion, they show understanding of the main points. Through relevant comments and questions, they show they have listened carefully. They begin to adapt what they say to the needs of the listener, varying the use of vocabulary and the level of detail. They are beginning to be aware of Standard English and when it is used.	• Can understand main points from discussion and respond to them • Able to recount the content of a presentation or discussion • Use vocabulary appropriate to subject, although it may not be very wide • Try to be adventurous but may sometimes misjudge vocabulary choice • Can ask relevant questions and make comments • Beginning to know the difference between Standard English and other dialects	• Continue to respond positively and constructively • May still need to offer support with new or unfamiliar concepts and vocabulary • Be explicit about the contexts in which standard English and other dialects are used • Discuss synonyms and other vocabulary choices looking at differences in use and meaning

Reading	Pupils read a range of texts fluently and accurately. They read independently using strategies appropriately to establish meaning. In responding to fiction and non-fiction they show understanding of the main points and express preferences. They use their knowledge of the alphabet to locate books and find information.	• Can read a range of age- appropriate text and understand most of what they read.
		• Can make simple inferences from the text.
		• Can choose leisure reading they enjoy and say why.
		• Can coordinate a range of reading strategies to read for understanding.
		• Can use the alphabet to access reference materials, e.g. indexes and encyclopaedias
			• Encourage pupils to identify vocabulary, phrases, expressions or idiom which they do not understand
			• Recognize that pupils might wish to read younger repetitive text for pleasure. This is a useful way of developing fluency and understanding
			• Support all use of references materials by:
			  – modelling note-taking
			  – limiting the research questions
			  – limiting the range of texts used

Skill	QCA/EAL statement	What the pupil can do at this level	Teacher strategies to help pupils move on
Writing	Pupils' writing is often organized, imaginative and clear. The main features of different forms of writing are used appropriately, beginning to be adapted to different readers. Sequences of sentences extend ideas logically and words are chosen for variety and interest. The basic grammatical structure of sentences is usually correct. Spelling is usually accurate, including that of common, polysyllabic words. Punctuation to mark sentences – full stops, capital letters and question-marks – is used correctly. Handwriting is joined and legible.	• Beginning to compose different forms of writing for different audiences • Can structure writing showing a logical progression of ideas • Can use some tenses accurately, e.g. simple past and simple present • Beginning to make a conscious choice of different vocabulary • Many pupils' work will show minor grammatical errors, e.g. in tense, use of pronouns, use of prepositions • Growing sight vocabulary, but will spell many words phonetically • Handwriting is legible but may not be joined unless this has been explicitly taught	• Make good use of scaffolding • Help the pupil to structure text cohesively, e.g. through consistent use of pronouns, time-sequencing, etc. • Embed use of key words in writing through shared writing • Discuss word roots and families • In marking or discussing written work, always respond to the content of the piece before commenting on presentation • Do not over correct, but choose one or two technical issues which are common errors in the writing

Level 4

NB: Many more advanced bilingual learners 'plateau' at this level. The overall aim for teachers should be to extend the range of vocabulary and structures across the four skills, e.g. by maximizing opportunities for language development through oral and written scaffolding and full, positive response to pupils' work

Skill	QCA/EAL statement	What the pupil can do at this level	Teacher strategies to help pupils move on
Speaking and Listening	Pupils talk and listen with confidence in an increasing range of contexts. Their talk is adapted to the purpose: developing ideas thoughtfully; describing events; and conveying their opinions clearly. In discussion, they listen carefully, making contributions and asking questions that are responsive to others' ideas and views. They use appropriately some of the features of standard English vocabulary and grammar.	• Can choose from a range of vocabulary and structures for different purposes and for emphasis • Can vary expression and speed of delivery for effect • Can follow an extended discussion or presentation but may have difficulty with idiom and cultural nuances • Responds to others' ideas and views by expressing alternative and personal opinions	• Make the aim of group/ pair discussion very clear, i.e. are pupils being asked to persuade, collaborate, debate or advise? • Make explicit the forms of language they are being expected to use • Use role-play and discuss the forms of language used by particular people, e.g. scientist, businessman, farmer and consumer discussing GM crops • Use formal debate • Use thinking time for responses and encourage collaboration for building on answers
Reading	In responding to a range of texts, pupils show understanding of significant ideas, themes, events and characters. They begin to use inference and deduction. They refer to the text when explaining their views. They locate and use ideas and information.	• Can read a range of age-appropriate texts and understand the important ideas, themes, events and characters • Are beginning to interrogate text – agreeing, disagreeing, developing ideas • Can show clear reasoning • Can show personal interpretation of information or personal voice in narrative • Can make links with other texts they have read	• Use grids, etc. to help develop ideas from text • Teach explicitly to use quotations from text as evidence for an argument • Teach explicitly how to summarize particular points from a text • Causes and consequences of human actions are culturally based. Pupils need support in understanding the cultural context when they are asked to make inferences and deductions

Skill	QCA/EAL statement	What the pupil can do at this level	Teacher strategies to help pupils move on
Writing	Pupils' writing in a range of forms is lively and thoughtful. Ideas are often sustained and developed in interesting ways and organized appropriately for the purpose of the reader. Vocabulary choices are often adventurous and words used for effect. Pupils are beginning to use grammatically complex sentences, extending meaning. Spelling, including that of polysyllabic words that conform to regular patterns, is generally accurate. Full stops, capital letters and question-marks are used correctly, and pupils are beginning to use punctuation within the sentence. Handwriting style is fluent, joined and legible.	• Can use text structure, particularly paragraphing, to suit the purpose of the text • Can use a variety of complex sentences, usually correctly • Can use a growing number of tenses appropriately and usually correctly. This would include present and past simple, present and past continuous and conditional • Spelling of longer words is becoming accurate • Basic punctuation is accurate • Beginning to use the comma	• Gradually introduce a range of different connectives, e.g. 'so that', 'although', 'despite', to help pupils write complex sentences • Model and develop complex sentences in shared writing • Discuss purpose of writing before starting shared writing or supporting independent writing • Ask pupil to read back writing in appropriate tone of voice • Continue to use a thesaurus and discuss the effect of vocabulary choices • Model more complicated tense forms in discussion before writing • In marking or discussing written work, continue to focus on content before forms of expression or grammar • Take opportunities to explore culturally based interpretations and implications

Bibliography

Bennett, H. (2006) *The Trainee Teacher's Survival Guide.* London: Continuum

Canter, L. (1992) *Assertive Discipline.* Santa Monica: Lee Canter and Associates

Dixie, G. (2005) *Getting on With Kids in Secondary Schools.* Dereham: Peter Francis

Dixie, G. (2007) *Managing Your Classroom.* London: Continuum.

Furlong, J. and Maynard, T. (1995) *Mentoring Student Teachers.* London: Routledge.

Gardner, H. (1993) Multiple Intelligences: *The Theory in Practice.* New York: Basic Books

Keddie, N. (1976) *Tinker, Taylor ... the Myth of Cultural Deprivation.* Harmonsworth: Penguin.

Leibling, M. and Prior, R. (2005) *The A–Z of Learning.* Abingdon: Routledge and Falmer

Lewis, M. (Ed.) (1998) *The Bristol Guide: Professional Responsibilities and Statutory Frameworks for Teachers and Others in Schools.* Bristol: Bristol University

Marland M. and Rogers R. (2004) *How to be a Successful Form Tutor* London: Continuum

Rist, R. (1970) 'Student social class and teacher expectations: the self-fulfilling prophecy in ghetto educations', *Harvard Educational Review.* 40.

Rogers, B. (1998) *You Know the Fair Rule.* London: Pitman.

Shaw, S. and Hawes, T. (1998) Effective Teaching and Learning in the Primary Classroom. Leicester: Optimal Learning.

Schön, D. (1983) *The Reflective Practitioner.* New York: Basic Books

Schön, D. (1987) *Educating the Reflective Practitioner: Towards a New Design for Teaching and Learning.* Indianapolis: Jossey-Bass Inc.

Schon, D. (1991) *The Reflective Turn.* New York: Teachers College Press

Zimpher, N. and Howey, K. (1987) 'Adapting supervisory practices to different orientations of teaching competence', *Journal of Curriculum and Supervision*. Winter, 2, 104–7.

The Literacy Skills Test. J. Johnson 2003 Exeter: Learning Matters

The ICT Skills Test. C. Ferrigan 2004 Exeter: Learning Matters

The Numeracy Skills Test. M. Patmore 2004 Exeter: Learning Matters

Websites

TDA (2008) *Support for ICT in ITT* [online] Available from http://www.tda.gov.uk/partners/quality/ict/supportforictinitt.aspx (accessed 11 June 2009)

Centre for Studies on Inclusive Education (2009) [online] Available from http://inclusion.uwe.ac.uk/csie/csiefaqs.htm (accessed 11 June 2009)

Encyclopaedia of Informal Education [online] Available form http://www.infed.org (accessed 11 June 2009)